happiness
happens

happiness
happens

a 10-week guide
to reconnect with who you are,
dream a new dream & make magic happen!

EMILY CAPURIA
LISW-S, CHHC

Printed in the United States of America

First Printing, 2018

Hardcover ISBN: 978-1-7329890-0-9

Balance & Thrive Publishing
PO Box 49
Willoughby, OH 44096

Cover and book layout design by Susana Cardona Ortega (susanacardona.es)
Cover and author photograph by Julie Stanley

This publication is not intended as a substitute for the advice of healthcare professionals. The author does not dispense medical advice or prescribe the use of any technique as a form of treatment for physical, emotional, or medical problems without the advice of a physician, either directly or indirectly. The information provided by this author is done so to offer information of a general nature to help you in your quest for happiness. In the event you use any of the information in this book for yourself, the author and the publisher assume no responsibility for your actions. If you have any specific questions about any medical matter, please consult your physician or healthcare professional.

To Mark...
your love and support gave me the courage
to become who I am and to go for my dreams.
Thank you does not even begin to do that justice.

xox

Contents

Before You Begin

This book was written to walk you through a process of self-discovery in a way that *feels manageable*—2 weeks at a time over a 10-week period. It was designed so that you can truly see what's available to you—_what's possible for you_—as of this moment. And it was designed in a way that lets you be who you truly are starting right now—without all the fight, resistance, fear and drama.

The timeline and results may vary for each individual person. But if you show up and engage 100 percent, you will notice something new and different. Something better than you could have ever imagined.

A LITTLE BACKGROUND

Like most people, I know what it's like to struggle at some point in my life. And while the details of our stories may be different, the themes are probably versions of the same.

For a really long time, I carried around this feeling that I was different and didn't belong. That there was something wrong with me. And this theme kept playing out in different ways in my life.

It made things feel confusing and hard. It led me to make a lot of decisions that took me far, far away from the true me. I felt angry for a long time. And there's about a decade of my life I once wished I could do over.

But life do-overs aren't a real thing. So I had to face my shit, find a way to forgive myself, and take the steps to truly move on. *I had to find a way back to me,* which started with me being okay with who I'd become, and accept the mess I had created within myself, which was also being expressed in pretty much every area of my life.

What I had wanted all along was actually quite simple: to just feel good and to be happy. When you really break it down, I think that's all any one of us is really looking for.

Sure, we might have different ideas of what exactly "feeling good" and "being happy" means, but *we're all wanting some version of that feel good/be happy theme*. We want to feel good in our bodies, in who we are and in how we're living. We want to belong, to be part of something and to see the meaning and value in ourselves and in our lives. And we want to smile, to be happy, to feel connected and to enjoy things. Regardless of what your specific version of happiness is, it'll always break down to be some form of a real-life expression of who you truly are.

When I say "accept," what I mean is to find peace with, to let it be what it is, and to stop with all the guilt and self-shaming. It's really easy to let those past regrets become a personal prison/way to hate yourself. Don't do that. It's a nightmare and a sure way to spiral even more. I say that from personal experience. See the conflict, let it show you what you want, and act accordingly. Don't get caught up in all the drama!

DEFINING HAPPINESS

Happiness happens when who you are, what you want and how you live are all in sync. And it happens when you decide it happens.

If your life isn't going the way you want it to, you've got to be willing to dig in and to look inside. At first, this might actually feel harder than keeping things as they are. Going within, facing all your personal dark and twisty stuff, and then changing, forgiving, letting go and taking those steps forward—it can get messy, it can be complicated and it can feel really, really hard. *Willingly stepping into all of this can seem a little crazy.* I get it.

For me, it wasn't until 2 years in to dealing with my "unexplained infertility" diagnosis (and following a devastating miscarriage at 14 weeks) that "keeping things as they are" became so much harder than changing.

I was tired of "being strong," which actually meant putting on a brave face, keeping everything inside, not telling the truth, not asking for help, and exploding at the wrong things. I could build up more walls to continue to hide the fact that *I felt completely broken.*

Or I could just tear them all down. I could let myself *be* broken. To feel it. To look into allllllllll that darkness. And to lean on the people in my life to ask for help so I could put the pieces back together in a new and different way. In a way, that let me be okay with the mess. To feel it all. To not have to pretend. And to not give a flying f*ck about keeping it together or pretending that everything was all sunshine, rainbows and roses.

I took a chance and decided to do things differently, which ultimately led me to feeling so much more like myself. *And it was amazing that as I changed, every single area of my life just naturally started to line up.* Yes, it required work (aka intentional effort), but *it all felt right and really, really worth it*, even in the moments when I couldn't say for sure that everything was going to work out the way I wanted it to.

The purpose of this book is to help you do the same. To **reconnect** with who you truly are and to **put your pieces together** in a way that lets you live your life so that it feels exactly right to *you*. Because *you matter.* **Your happiness matters.** And now is the perfect time to do something about it.

The Purpose of this Book

It wasn't until I accepted me for me, and my life as it was at the time, that I was able to see my value and strength. Everyone isn't going to like me or agree with me and that's okay (now)—I don't need them to. *We all do life in our own way* and that's fine (it's actually great because it makes our world dynamic and interesting).

Life can be hard and messy sometimes, but for the most part, it's really, really good. The hard and messy times don't negate the good—they're actually part of each other.

Once you get this, everything starts to change. The "big deal" things that don't actually mean anything stop meaning everything. And the simple, little things you've been missing out on, but that are *actually the fabric of your life*, become the important things you focus on.

Simple shifts happen. Then, one day, you wake up different, feeling more like yourself than ever before, *without actually having to remember to do things differently*.

There are way too many people suffering and feeling alone. They're believing that there is something wrong with them because life feels hard, messy and imperfect. And it's simply not true.

A happy life is accessible to everyone. And everyone is deserving of it, worthy of it and can absolutely make it happen. And when we step into this belief, we become evidence for others that this is possible for them, too. *We get to show, support, share, celebrate and inspire each other along the way.* That's actually one of the best parts.

This is the kind of world I want my son to grow up in—one that feels safe, and where the people in it are happy and kind. I want him to live a life that's mostly good, even if it's not always fair. I want him to see that life can be hard sometimes, but that it's really amazing, too. I want him to know that he is loved for exactly who he is, that he is strong, and that his heart knows best, but he has to learn to tune in to and trust in that, and to turn off all the other noise. I want him to have the opportunity to really experience life at its fullest.

These are the exact same things I want for you, too.

The whole point of life is to show up, to do your best, to be who you are and to really live life in your own way. In this book, I will teach you how to do that by giving you pieces of short, easy-to-grasp information, ideas on first steps you can take right now, and writing prompts to explore your thoughts and perspective on things.

I will walk you through a process of self-discovery. You will have the opportunity to challenge the whole operating system that you're working with right now. Your thoughts, beliefs and past experiences are the foundation for who you are and how you live today.

But that foundation can change. Right now, you recognize that something doesn't feel quite right. How many times have you thought to yourself, "There's got to be more to life than this"? Because you know deep down, _you are meant for more_.

I wrote this book to help you prove what you already know deep down is true. I will help you sort through all of your stuff so that you can create a new foundation and start to live your life in a way that feels exactly right to you. So that you feel fulfilled, see your purpose *and live your more*.

You'll finally cut through all of the b.s. so you can see what you want and know what you're willing to do to get there. You'll finally get rid of all the stuff that doesn't work. And, most importantly, you'll have a little fun along the way!

How to Use this Book

Several years ago, I decided to have the two tattoos on my back removed. When I went to the hospital for the first procedure (yes, this was years ago when they did it in the hospital, old-school style), the surgeon described the removal process like *breaking up a boulder.*

He told me to imagine a giant boulder. When he shoots the laser in, it breaks the boulder (the ink) into smaller pieces. Then, he has to go in and shoot those smaller pieces with the laser to break them down some more. He has to do this over and over again until the pieces are so small I can no longer see them. For me, this was 21 times—yikes!

This book is like that. *Over each 2-week period, you're going at the same bottom line in 14 different, yet similar ways.* You're breaking down your boulder into small manageable pieces **so you can get to** the bottom line. So you can hold it, feel it, integrate it, and live it.

Sometimes, we need to *hear* things, *do* things and *look* at things **in different ways and from different angles** in order to get to that bottom line. You want the pieces you're working with to *feel* really manageable so that *what you're doing feels doable, is effective and you'll stick with it!*

THE STEPS

Over 10 weeks, you'll move through 5 steps:

1. Reigniting Your Dreams
2. Becoming You
3. Letting Go
4. Bringing It to Life
5. Being Happy Anyway

Focus on one step at a time for 2 weeks; do one thing each day. Go through the information, digest it, and take the action. *At the end of each step, <u>decide on one new insight and one or two new actions to continue.</u>*

Do each of the exercises in the book *at least once.* Try the one for that day so you can apply what you learned, and then *decide to keep it or leave it.* You <u>*don't*</u> want to end up with a monster "happiness to-do list;" it'll become overwhelming and not at all sustainable! ***Trust that you'll get exactly what you need when you need it.*** Don't try to do everything all the time. This book is yours to keep. You can come back to it at anytime and as often as you'd like!

The steps are organized based on the process I most commonly walk my clients through. I've found that people often need to *reconnect* with who they are, start to *dream* again so that they can *see* what's in conflict with those pieces, and then *decide* what they need to let go. However, it's not uncommon for people to want to start with "Letting Go." Sometimes, you have to clear the field before you can plant the seed. If that feels right for you, go for it!

I've also found that while you think you can just cut straight to "Being Happy Anyway," *it's actually really hard to make the decision to be happy anyway without going through the other steps first.* It's the entire process (of reconnecting with who you are, of dreaming a new dream, of letting go, and of doing your part) *that makes it possible for you* to be happy anyway. It's also a process of redefining what happiness actually means to you. Coming up with a new, true-to-you definition usually requires at least a little bit of the self-discovery.

When you know who you are, when you trust in what you're doing and when you're okay with how things come together, that's "how" you can be happy living a messy, imperfect life.

Everyone is different and you get to decide where this experience starts for you. If you start somewhere other than Step 1, that's fine. Just *be sure to work your way through all of the steps* in whatever order makes the most sense to you.

Don't rush through it, but don't dillydally either. *You bought this book for a reason* and it wasn't so it could just sit on your shelf!

Get ready for your perspective, your way of thinking and how you live your life to completely change. Hang on and enjoy this amazing ride! And bring some friends along with you, too! Read the "Book Club It" section for ideas about how to read and discuss this book with your book club or group of friends.

A FEW MORE THINGS

This book is written in a conversational tone because *it's meant to be a conversation.* Throw it in your bag so you can engage in the conversation whenever you feel like it. Pull it out at brunch with the girls or at dinner with your sister. Talk about *all of* the things!!!

Agree. Disagree. Love it. Leave it. It doesn't matter—*there is no right or wrong.* This is an opportunity to get triggered, to get curious, to get excited and to _use it all_!!! **The only thing that really matters is that you get engaged!**

Get a pen you love—take notes, brainstorm, doodle, think, reflect and _do it all in this book as you go_.

Write in the margins. Circle, underline and highlight things. Play with it, work with it, and use it to formulate your perspective, to poke holes in your blind spots, and to consider new ideas and new ways of doing things.

Each segment gives you information to consider, an action to take and the space to reflect on it. **The more you engage with _all_ the pieces, the more you'll get out of the experience.** Play with the content in here and mold it to you, _not_ you to it!

You are absolutely allowed to love or leave whatever you want. Feel free to disagree with things. And just because I say it doesn't make it true for you. Use it all to find _what is true for you_. A line may spark a new idea, insight or inspiration—go with it. Let that flow, and see where it takes you. This is all about _you getting what you need_. It's about your journey so make it work for you.

WHEN YOU'RE READY FOR MORE

Happiness Happens is one important step in the big picture. The insights you gain and the new actions you take are invaluable, and they truly have the potential to **completely transform every area of your life in a way that feels exactly right and completely natural.**

As you pull back these layers, you may start to see that you're ready for what's next, for something bigger. And your "what's next" could be a dream that you didn't even realize you had. My surprise dream was Balance & Thrive, the business I started in 2012.

Big goals and dreams are best achieved with support, practical step-by-step strategies and accountability—a framework to help you get from point A to point B. That's where the "Laugh More, Live Louder" course comes in.

This is a year-long online course that's broken up into 4 phases to match the seasons. There's a season for everything, and when you learn how to match your action to your energy, and the energy of the season you're in, you'll not only maximize your productivity (the results of your action) but you'll also feel happier every step of the way. You'll be doing the things to get you to where you want to go AND you'll be getting to where you want to be.

You can read more about the course, why it's structured the way it is and how it can help you in the *What's Next?* section or, head over to balancethrive.com/laughmorelivelouder.

A FINAL NOTE BEFORE YOU BEGIN

Thank you for being the kind of person who's brave enough to show up for yourself, to decide that *your life matters,* and to *do all the things you can* to make it count.

You're an inspiration who is making this world a better place for all of us, and even though we may not know each other personally, I love you for that!

I can't wait to hear how it goes for you. Be sure to tag me @ balancethrive in anything you post on social media (I most often hang out on Instagram and Facebook). And I always welcome personal emails—I read every single one!

Here's to you making *your* happiness happen!

Emily xox

1

STEP ONE

Reigniting
Your Dreams

Turn on

Tune in

Feel

Imagine

Want

Wish

Reignite

Dream

Introduction

As a kid, I dreamed of being Madonna. Or Baby from Dirty Dancing. And in high school, I wished I could be one of the Spice Girls, but I lacked the skill set to get me there. The closest I ever got was lip-syncing "Love You I Do" (from the movie Dreamgirls) to Mark at our wedding reception. It was awesome!

Now, I mostly just sing and dance in the kitchen with my family on Saturday mornings. Or at weddings...

I went to Law School once. That was a dream I thought I had, but one year ended up being waaaaay more than enough! I went because of the things I was good at, and who I thought I wanted to be—but it just never clicked. Honestly, it was a terrible fit. And the timing was off. I now know that dream was never really meant for me anyway.

Dreams are funny. We have *a lot* of them throughout our lifetime. Some of them come true; some of them don't. Me not becoming a singer, dancer or movie star—no big deal. Me not becoming an attorney—outside of the school loans, I'm just grateful that wasn't my long-term path.

But then there are those dreams, *maybe one or two*, that paralyze you when they don't happen or they fall apart. It may even be a dream you didn't even realize you had...until it didn't come true!

Maybe you dreamed of a passion-filled career, but just never got that dream job. So, you stepped into something that was fine and 25 years later, you're still there! Maybe you found your one true love and dreamed of building a life together, but for whatever reason, it never quite came together, or it all fell apart. Heartache like that is brutal. You just couldn't risk it, but now you're feeling kinda lonely.

The dreams of yours that didn't come true may have been about missed opportunities. Or about someone you loved leaving your life way too soon. Maybe it was about assuming life would just work out in a certain way one day, never once considering that it wouldn't. And maybe it's about something completely different, but I know you know exactly what I'm talking about. *It's that dream that's come to mind for you right now.*

I never really realized that I had a dream of becoming a mom until it wasn't happening. I guess I had always had it in my heart, but never in my head. Once I had stepped into that dream and felt how important it was to me, it was devastating to be disappointed every 28 days, for 7 years.

The hardest part of that journey was in 2009 when I miscarried at 14 weeks. The moment I found out I was pregnant, I fell instantly in love. The moment I found out my baby's heart had stopped beating, I felt completely broken. This was 2 years in to what ended up being a 7-year struggle with unexplained infertility.

It was a dream that had become paralyzing and all-consuming. And while it wasn't until a few years later that things really shifted, that loss was a turning point for me. I don't believe it happened for a reason, but I do believe I gave reason—*purpose and meaning*—to it happening.

Everything in my life now came from that place of loss. That place of being broken. That place of knowing that if I wanted to survive the pain of a miscarriage and unexplained infertility,

I had to create something that gave my life, and this journey I was on, meaning.

It was a process, of course. It took years. I didn't go from that loss to instantly realizing I wanted to start Balance & Thrive and I certainly didn't see myself sitting here writing this book to you. But I did know that I needed to change how I was doing things. *I needed to let myself feel excited, interested, engaged, passionate, vulnerable and hopeful.* I needed a way to survive this thing <u>and</u> to find some level of happiness, too. I needed to find a way to let it all coexist. To be happy, to be sad and to be everything in-between (some days even all at the same time).

Because if I didn't, I knew I was at risk of forever being completely consumed by this dream of becoming a mom. In the deepest part of my being, I knew that I was meant to be a mom, but the evidence I was getting in my life was telling me something completely different. I needed to be able to hope and to act, but to *also* live a happy and fulfilling life. Because while this dream was incredibly important, it was not the only dream I had.

So, what I did was I tapped into some of those other dreams. I gave myself the opportunity to be happy anyway—no matter what. And I just kept taking a series of next best steps. I feel immensely grateful (and quite honestly, very lucky) with how things came together for me. This first section is intended to help you with this process for yourself.

The information, actions and reflection prompts are the how-tos of dreaming a new dream. *They will lead you to those wishes, wants, dreams and desires that are lying dormant inside of you.* The ones that have been, for whatever reason, pushed aside. This is your chance to give yourself the opportunity to be happy now, no matter what. And to discover your next best steps so that a new version of happiness happens for you, too!

I. THERE'S STILL TIME! IT'S NOT TOO LATE. No matter what your age, where you've been or what you've been through, there's absolutely still time for you to dream a new dream and to create a life filled with what makes you happy.

But, it will require your willingness to let go and to take action.

Things may not look how you thought they would. Regrets, past disappointments, unmet expectations—you've got 'em, but they don't define you. And they don't define your life.

Your ship hasn't sailed. It's just waiting for you to come aboard, decide to step on—ready or not—and to take the wheel.

Yes, there is still time for you to be happy, to feel alive, and to do the things you want to do. *There is so much possibility that awaits you.*

It's absolutely not too late.

There are new dreams, wishes, wants and desires brewing deep inside of you. Let them out. Bring them to life.

Be willing to dream your new dream. To create, believe in and step into a different version of happiness.

There is so much beauty in this phase that you're in, so much joy to be had, and so much life to live. You've just got to be willing to see it and to say yes to it. To let it be what it is. To let it be enough.

It's time to dream a new dream. To shed the old one. The one you've been secretly holding on to, even though it's long gone. Grieve it. Get mad about it. And then send it on its way.

It's time. Right now.

Give yourself a fresh start. *A new vision based on who you are as of this moment.* Dream from this place. Create from here. And let yourself be amazed at all the things there's still plenty of time for in your life.

DO THIS

Imagine yourself walking down into a deep, deep valley. It's beautiful, filled with lush greenery. You feel completely safe, comfortable and at home here.

As you reach the bottom of the valley, see yourself approach a beautiful pond filled with crystal clear water. It reminds you of a wishing well.

Imagine yourself sitting down at the edge of the water. Look at your reflection and smile. See the beauty, the meaning and the wisdom looking back at you.

As you sit there smiling and appreciating where you are, ask yourself to let all of your right now wishes, wants and desires be reflected back to you.

Notice as some of your wishes, wants and desires are ones you've been carrying around with you for a long time and some are brand new. Notice as some feel a little exciting; others, a little scary; and most, a little of both.

Just let them all come to you. Let them bubble to the surface.

Sit with the beauty, meaning and wisdom that's inside of you. Let it show you what's next for you. It could be a feeling, an image, or something very specific.

Write down what comes to you.

My wishes, new dreams and what's next for me (examples):

- to be happy
- find someone to share my life with
- Start a book club—and really talk about things that matter
- Maybe a pet…
- Volunteer—help kids learn to read
- A career that lets me actually see the results of the work I put in!
-
-
-
-
-
-
-
-
-
-

*** For a visualization to help you with this, visit balancethrive.com/hhdownloads***

WRITE HERE:

There's still time for you, this is absolutely true. How does this statement / thought / belief feel for you? What about it feels exciting, scary, or overwhelming? What feels at greatest risk for you in thinking about dreaming a new dream?

....

 2. FLIP YOUR SWITCH BACK ON. It's time to reconnect with the part of you that wants, desires, dreams and imagines. The part of you that creates.

It's time to come back to the part of you that takes risks, embraces life and truly believes that _anything is possible._ The part of you that feels and trusts.

It's time to put the heart of who you are _back_ in the driver's seat. The part of you that's simultaneously vulnerable and strong. That's curious and full of wisdom. And that knows in her core exactly who she is and what she wants.

This part of you has always been there. You were born with it. It is you. It's the essence of who you are. And it connects you to everything—to yourself, to others, and to your life.

And it's all lying dormant, *waiting for you* to flip that switch back on. To finally let yourself dream again. To feel again. To get back in the game.

Life happened. It took you off course. It's okay.

Then one day, you woke up, looked in the mirror and wondered *how exactly you got here.* How did you end up living a life of just going through the motions? At what point did you tune out and turn off?

But those details don't really matter. What matters is that you miss that part of you. The part of you that feels so natural and right. That walks with confidence and knows exactly what to do.

You miss your curiosity, excitement and anticipation. You miss your light. And you miss feeling really, really alive.

So now, it's time to relight that fire inside of you. To reconnect with your passion and to refuel your inspiration. *It all starts the moment you decide to flip that switch back on.*

Look closely: you'll see that the sparkle is still in your eyes. That what lights you up still lives inside of you. Just *give yourself permission* to tap back in, to turn back on and to truly feel it all.

Turn the key. Rev the engine. Go for a ride. And let how you feel guide every step of the way.

DO THIS

Get back into your body. Tune into how things feel for you.

Think about what inspires you, makes you smile, and gives you goosebumps. How do you *physically feel* when you're around

---

these things? What gets you excited, makes your heart race and your cheeks flush? Start to really *pay attention to how experiences feel in your body.*

Do the things that light you up and <u>feel</u> the excitement in your body.

Generate a list of people, places, ideas, experiences, etc. that light you up. As you bring each one to mind, check in with your body. How does it physically feel?

What lights me up:	How it physically feels:
• Bright, beautiful sunsets	• Takes my breath away, in awe
• The ocean	• Peaceful & connected
• People I love	• Smile, heart feels full
• Music	• Depends on the song—but I always feel it in my body, my soul—deep in my bones & I can't help but move!

The more of these things you experience, the more you'll feel that switch inside of you flip back on.

*** *For a visualization to help you with this, visit balancethrive.com/hhdownloads* ***

WRITE HERE:

Generally speaking, do you feel connected to or disconnected from your body? In what ways? What's it like for you to take a moment and to really pay attention to how things *actually feel* in your body? Does the idea of being in your body feel comfortable or uncomfortable to you?

....

 3. YOUR LIFE IS MEANT TO BE LIVED AS A BEAUTIFUL EXPRESSION OF WHO YOU ARE. When you know who you are and what matters to you most, you can live those things *out loud* every single day. You can fill your life with all that lights you up, makes you smile and gives you pleasure. You can use your strengths and follow your passions.

You can bring who you are to life
by how you live!

It's like painting a picture or creating anything really. You do it as an expression of a piece of you. Some days, your picture might be all dark and twisty. Some days, it might be all sunshine and roses. Some days, it might be some wild and crazy combination of both.

Regardless, it's always a *true expression* of you. So, it feels good. It feels right.

You don't question or doubt it. You look at it and feel at peace. You feel happy seeing who you are expressed in this way. This is what life is all about!

There's nothing more fulfilling than being able to *create and live your life* on your terms. As you want. WIth your priorities and values being at the center of it all.

It starts with reconnecting with who you are. With shedding all those expectations, those people-pleasing behaviors and those dreams that don't belong to you.

It's about reclaiming your passion.
And letting your light set your life on fire!

So as of right now, stop seeking, wondering and feeling lost. Stop letting the question "What do I want?" be the hardest question you have to answer. And stop trying to live a life that doesn't belong to you.

Get quiet and still. Breathe and just be. *Start to feel the dreams and the parts of you that were silenced along the way.* Start to hear all of your answers that are already there. Hear that little voice inside of you get stronger, louder and more confident.

Give her all the power back. She knows you best. She is you. And when you let her be heard, when you quiet all the noise and distraction, *she will show you the way.*

DO THIS

Sit down, close your eyes, and be still. Put your hands on your heart. Breathe in and out at a slow, steady, rhythmic pace.

Notice what you hear, smell and feel. Do this for 10 breaths.

It's the first step in letting you truly express yourself. **You have to be able to hear your heart before you can speak your truth.**

Now, get creative: paint, journal, knit, cook, garden, scrapbook. Whatever you LOVE to do to create, do that now.

If you need a little time to plan or prepare, no problem! Go ahead and do that first.

I want to be creative by... (examples):

- Journaling—free writing always helps me to put into words what I'm thinking and feeling.
- Scrapbooking—I love taking pictures, quotes and things I find in nature to create a collage of a memory, something I want or even as a gift—it just helps me pull in all of these different pieces of me.

- _____ - _____

- _____ - _____

What I need to make it happen (examples):

- notebook w/ unlined paper
- Some colorful gel pens I love
- Pictures & things that inspire (& that I can glue down)
- 15 minutes of quiet time each morning

- _____ - _____

- _____ - _____

WRITE HERE:

What are some of the ways you can *express who you are by how you live?* What can you create that truly expresses a part of you? What about this feels most exciting to you? What feels the scariest?

....

 4. YOUR DREAMS ARE THERE, BUT MAY BE HIDING. Remember those things you used to get so excited just thinking about, but stopped because it got too hard? Or someone told you it was stupid, silly, unimportant, not for you or that you couldn't do it?

Those things you stuffed down,
even though they lit you up.

You actually started to believe all those naysayers (odds are, you were the loudest one of all). "I'm not good enough, smart enough, young enough, strong enough, enough enough" or "I'm too young, too old, too fat, too busy, too broke, too tired, too whatever."

And you checked out. *Because if you can't do the things that make your heart happy, what's the point?* You settled in to a life that's "fine" but you actually feel restless, disconnected and bored.

Here's the thing: the best things in life aren't the easiest. *Yes, there is a sense of ease when something's right for you, but that doesn't mean no grit is required, or that it won't ever be hard.*

You'll be tired, overwhelmed and lost sometimes. BUT you'll love whatever it is you're doing so much that it won't even matter. You'll keep on going with a smile in your heart.

You won't care what people say or how so-and-so does it because you will be so sure in how <u>you</u> are doing it. It's what you believe in and you'll let that faith, passion and drive lead the way.

If you're not feeling that way about what you're doing right now, you're chasing the wrong dream. You're going for a "safe" version of what you want so that you don't have to go full out and risk falling on your face and feeling awful.

But you've got to get to the good stuff. The stuff that feels both insanely exciting and WTF-level scary. And you've got to let those bad boys out. Let them breathe and expand and turn back into your dreams.

Tick tock, my friend. Your life is waiting!

DO THIS

Think about who you once dreamed of being. If you were to reignite that vision, what parts of you would turn back on? What would you start doing that you once stopped? How could you express these parts in your life today?

Generate a list of all the different ways that come to you. Then, choose one to try today. Even if it seems silly, <u>do it anyway</u>.

Example:

I once dreamed of being a singer, but was always told that I can't sing so I stopped ALL singing. Today, I'm going to start singing again. Wherever and whenever I can—in the shower, as I get ready for work, in the car—I might even go to Karaoke tonight!

And I'll remember that this is for me, and it's all in fun. I'll look for all the different ways I can reignite my love for all things music (singing included). Hey maybe I can dance on one of those piano mats like in the movie Big!!!

One thing I can, want to and will do today to express this part of me is:

WRITE HERE:

What thoughts and feelings come up for you when you think about expressing this part of you that's been silenced for so long? Do you want to bring more of this part of you to life? Why or why not? And if yes, in what ways?

5. WHO YOU ARE AND WHAT YOU WANT MATTERS—IT'S TOTALLY UP TO YOU TO LIVE LIKE IT. At some point in your life, you started to believe that who you are and what you want doesn't actually matter. It happens to the best of us. But it doesn't make it okay and it doesn't make it true.

It's time for you to <u>*step up and decide*</u> *differently.* To get back in the game and to become re-engaged in life. It's the best possible thing for you and all of your people. Now is the perfect time to get into action.

That means you ask for things. You set boundaries. You *value* who you are and what matters to you most. You do it every single day. And you watch as the truth of who you are starts to unfold.

You see the beauty and the power that <u>you</u> bring to the table. No one else can do you like you can. And the world needs you to show up!

When you value yourself first, when you live like you matter, that message will be received loud and clear. You'll be happier. The people in your life will be happier. And the world will benefit immensely from you finally showing up and making *you* count!

DO THIS

Today, commit to giving clear, concrete answers without justifying, rationalizing or apologizing.

Examples:
- I'd like spaghetti for dinner tonight.
- I'm in the mood to listen to some old school hip hop.
- Yes, let's go to the cute wine bar on the corner for happy hour.

Getting what you want in life is simply a series of knowing what you want and then acting accordingly (aka doing the things to make it happen). Practice *speaking up about what you want* as often as possible—it's one of the most important steps you can take.

Ask yourself: what do I want in this moment? (write whatever comes to you)

_____

_____

_____

What action(s) can I take right now to make it happen or, at least, move me closer to it?

_____

_____

_____

_____

WRITE HERE:

What are 5 things you want in your life. Do the actions you take on a daily basis match what you say you want? What do you need, and want, to change?

For example, if you say you want to lose 10 lbs, are you drinking mostly water (matching) or mostly coffee/pop (not matching), eating mostly whole foods, veggies, fruits, healthy fats, lean proteins, etc. (matching) or mostly take-out/processed foods or skipping meals completely (not matching)? Are you moving your body regularly/ exerting yourself (matching) or mostly sitting (not matching)?

••• *Here's a great journaling exercise: each morning, take 5-10 minutes to free-write. Start with a blank sheet of paper. In large letters at the top, write* **WHAT I WANT**... *and then, just write, write, write whatever comes to mind. As you write these wants, be sure to also include the daily actions that will help get you there.*•••

 6. LET WHAT YOU DON'T WANT POINT YOU TO WHAT YOU DO WANT. It's easy to talk about what you don't want. You see it, feel it and know it so strongly. But the magic happens when you can turn that around.

When you can let your "don't wants" show you *what you do want* instead. When you let them spark the truth of your hidden desires.

You'll never get to where you want to go if all you focus on is what you don't want.

But knowing those "don't wants"—feeling them and experiencing them—that serves an important purpose: it points you to what you *do want*. It shows you where to go.

Don't hide, ignore or shove all of that very valuable information down.

Let your likes and dislikes all be okay. It's natural and normal to have preferences about all sorts of things. The less judgmental you are towards yourself about having judgments, *the more those personal dislikes will be able to point you in your right direction.*

Let it be the fuel to your fire.

Let it ignite your dreams, and show you the way. Then, let all those don't wants fade away. They've served their purpose, and you're ready to move on.

DO THIS

In the left-hand column in the space below, write down all of the things happening in your life right now that you dislike or don't want.

Then, in the right-hand column under "do want," write at least one thing you'd like to experience instead.

It's okay to have multiple "do wants" per "don't want." Just be sure to have at least one.

Once you've completed your "do want" list, put a big X through the "don't want" column. Those are done now; no more energy or time needs to go there.

Shift your focus to your "do wants." And start checking them off as you go!

Don't want:	Do want:
Credit card debt	Completely debt-free
	Pay my bills each month with ease
	Have 6 months' worth of bills in savings
	Contribute regularly to my retirement fund
	Feel confident about my money
	Be financially savvy/educated

* * * *Notice how your "do wants" become actionable items. You can start to ask yourself "What can I do today to feel more confident with my finances or to become more educated about money?" This gives you something you <u>can do</u>, which helps you to feel more in control and less overwhelmed by the "don't want," in this case, the debt. Even if the number doesn't change right away, taking a class or speaking to a financial advisor helps you to know you're moving in the right direction and you'll feel better about the situation!* * * *

WRITE HERE:

What is it you actually <u>do</u> want? How does it feel to really own that? What's it like for you to be able to shift your focus in this way?

7. ONE OF THE BRAVEST THINGS YOU'LL EVER DO IS DARE TO DREAM ANOTHER DREAM. When you put so much of yourself into a dream and it doesn't come together, it's heartbreaking. You feel like you've lost a piece of yourself.

It's scary to think of going back there. *To risk so much of you* on something that's not guaranteed.

But there are no guarantees. So, you have to find a way.

Start by giving yourself permission to grieve that old dream— to feel the sadness and the disappointment. Give that part of you *every single thing it needs* and then, let go.

And let the letting go spark the new.

When you do this, you reclaim a piece of yourself. You feel the pain AND you step back into your power. You reconnect with the part of you that dares to dream, to imagine, to create, and to play. Without shutting any of you off.

This is the way to be brave. To feel alive. To be totally you. And to dream another dream.

DO THIS

Write down one dream that you poured so much of yourself into, but for whatever reason, it didn't come true. Notice any feelings that come up. Pick a song that's the perfect theme song for this dream, and how you feel about it. Write it down.

Play the song. Bring the dream to mind, feel it all and dance it out.

Decide that when the song's over, the dream, and everything about it that you've been holding on to, will be over, too.

Dream:	Song:
Being a mom	Fresh Eyes, Andy Grammer
Being a singer	I Love Rock 'n' Roll, Joan Jett
Backpacking through Europe	You Can't Always Get What You Want, Rolling Stones

••• *The songs on your list might be there because of the title, beat or lyrics. It could be about a time in your life, a message you need to be reminded of or a connection to a person who always helped you gain perspective. Or it could be a completely random "this just feels right" kind of reason. Don't worry about your personal playlist making sense. It doesn't need to. You just need to be able to feel in your body what you need to feel and let it do its thing. Trust your gut on this!* •••

WRITE HERE:

Put your dreams (past and present) to music. What's your playlist? How does it feel to put your dreams to music? In what ways can you use your playlist to help you reconnect with who you are, dream a new dream, let go of what's gone, become your true self and be happy anyway?

....

 8. YOUR PURPOSE IS TO LIVE ON PURPOSE. Yes, it truly is that simple. Slow down. Pay attention. Be present. And do as many things as you possibly can with intention.

So many people are searching for their purpose. But they're searching so much, they actually wind up missing it.

When you *stop searching and instead, you slow down and pay attention*, a whole new world opens up. You see things differently. You notice the details. You connect. And you live your purpose innately. It's a natural, fluid thing that just happens.

You are the one who gives purpose and meaning to your life. You decide what it is and what it means to you. It's <u>not</u> some predetermined thing that's supposed to be a big secret waiting to be revealed. *And it's certainly not meant to be kept a secret from you!*

But because you're so busy searching for what you think is hidden, you're missing what's right in front of you. It's the simplest of things that light you up inside. It's the things you're just naturally good at, that you assume are no big deal and everyone else can do. *That's your purpose.*

It's whatever feels second nature to you and completely natural. Having conversations with strangers everywhere you go. Whipping up an amazing meal. Volunteering to help kids read. It's what you do, and *enjoy*, on a very regular basis.

It's you living your life: showing up, doing your best and enjoying as much as you possibly can.

DO THIS

Below, number from 1 to 25. Brainstorm a list of the things that come easily to you, that you just naturally do. If you need help, ask your family, friends and colleagues. They're probably *regularly amazed* at how you do this thing—whatever it is—with such ease.

You're not limited to 25. Once you get going, new things might come to you. Feel free to come up with 100 or more!

From your list, circle what you get most excited about doing, what you love, and what you just simply find interesting. Think of things you get lost in or you could spend all day doing.

Then each day, do as many of the things on your list *with intention*. Meaning, choose it and notice when you do it.

Odds are, you don't even realize when you're doing these things. Once you start to pay attention, you'll see, and *feel*, a lot more connected to the purpose you're already living!

25 things that come easily or naturally to me (examples):

1. Patience
2. Writing
3. Cooking
4. Talking with strangers
5. Math
6. Seeing different sides of the same situation
7. Gardening
8.
9.
10.
11.
12.
13.
14.
15.
16.
17.
18.
19.
20.
21.
22.
23.
24.
25.

WRITE HERE:

Your purpose is what you love, enjoy, find interesting and are good at—that's it. How does it feel for you to think about your life purpose in this way? What new ideas do you now have about what your purpose is?

*** *To take this one step further, download the "Live Your Purpose" exercise at balancethrive.com/hhdownloads* ***

9. LET YOUR GRATITUDE SPARK YOUR DESIRE. You get to be grateful _AND_ you get to go for more.

It's not selfish or greedy. It doesn't undermine or discredit what you have. Those are just stories that limit your potential and all that's possible for you.

The more goodness you have, the more you have to give. So, let it grow!!!

Let all that's good and working in your life pull you forward. Let your gratitude spark your desires!

DO THIS

Today, practice your "and" (examples):

I'm grateful for my healthy body _AND_ I'm excited to push it to the next level by going to the Disney Marathon next year (even if I just do the 5k!).

I'm grateful for my job _AND_ I'd love to start my own business doing something similar (tech consulting maybe?).

I'm grateful for my kiddo _AND_ I'd love to have another baby.

Get comfortable appreciating what you have while also stretching yourself to what's next.

My list of "and's":

_____

_____

_____

_____

_____

WRITE HERE:

What's working in your life, and in what way might it also spark what's next for you? How does the experience of wanting more feel for you? What stories and beliefs do you have about wanting more (i.e. it's selfish or greedy, just be grateful, stay humble, etc.) that you need to change, shift or reframe?

....

 10. EVERYTHING YOU WANT IS A LOT CLOSER THAN YOU REALIZE. When you really start to look at what it is you want, and what having it will do for you, you'll start to see that *you already have some version of it in your life right now.*

And when you can see this, it becomes a lot easier to create more of it. It doesn't feel so hard or elusive.

It becomes this thing you've already got going for you in some way, and <u>now</u>, you simply have to expand it into the other areas of your life.

You have the foundation. You just have to *build on* what already exists. Bringing more of what you've already got into your life feels so much easier than starting completely from scratch.

DO THIS

Look at the thing, or things, you want. In what ways are they already showing up in your life?

Example: I want to be in a long-term relationship with someone who loves and supports me.

My mom, sister and pup show me so much love and support. Just yesterday, my sister called to ask how work was going. I loved that she thought of me, especially since work has been so stressful lately. My mom is always a really great listener and somehow gives me advice without me ever feeling like she's trying to fix anything. And Rocky is the best pup ever—always there ready to cuddle up with me. He somehow just knows exactly what I need and delivers without needing a single thing in return.

Seeing what you already have with current real-life examples helps you to know that **what you want is possible for you because it already exists in some way in your life right now.**

The more you start to see that you have the things you want, the more you'll get of what you want in new and different ways.

What I want: **Examples of how I already have it:**

....

....

....

....

....

WRITE HERE:

Does seeing that you already have some version of what you want in your life feel surprising to you? How can you use this awareness to bring more of what you want into your life?

....

II. GO AHEAD AND DREAM THAT MILLION-DOLLAR DREAM. You've got to be willing to go big. To let yourself really dream it. Play around. Imagine. And expand on the idea of what you could create.

Let yourself get excited and see *what's possible.*

Feel the spark of what you want in your bones—it's got to be that deep and powerful. Playing small won't cut it, so *make sure that what you want is powerful enough to push you to go all in,*

You've got to be able to feel it...in the depths of your soul. The core of your being.

Yes, you've been hurt at some point in your life in some way by some person.

Maybe it was someone you loved, like your mom or dad, a sibling, boyfriend or spouse who let you down or broke your trust. Maybe it was a teacher, mentor or boss who criticized you or made you feel insignificant or stupid. Or maybe it was your peers who judged or laughed at you.

And so, you made the decision to never let yourself feel that way again. You decided to protect yourself, no matter what, because pain like that is just too much.

You built up some walls and put on some armor. And then, somehow, it became you against the world. Keeping people at arm's length so that you can't be hurt again. Not getting your hopes up so you won't be disappointed. Ignoring what you actually want because it feels way too risky.

But you know what happens with all that work to protect yourself? *You actually end up blocking you from who you really are and what you actually want.* All of that truth gets buried—even from you. You shrink your dreams waaaaaaaay down. And what you actually want becomes your best-kept secret.

If you were to get totally honest about your hopes and dreams for you and your life—like selfishly, scarily, real, deep-down and raw honest—what would you see that maybe you don't want to see? What scary things would you have to face or endure?

Until you let yourself really go there, you're going to keep feeling stuck.

You deserve to not only dream, but to also go for your million-dollar dream. To see what you can create and to really go all in. It's probably really flipping scary because it's going to require you to do the very thing you've been protecting yourself from.

DO THIS

Remember as a kid how you'd just imagine and play? Do that now.

Let yourself imagine if you could have anything you wanted —anything at all—no limitations. No worries about it being important enough or possible. No worries about figuring out the logistics. And no worries about anyone being hurt or getting nasty or judgmental. What would you imagine? What would you let yourself dare to dream?

Today, spend 5-10 minutes letting your imagination take over. Play with your daydream. Reignite that part of you.

Some notes about what I dared to dream:

_____

_____

_____

_____

_____

*** *For a visualization to help you with this, visit balancethrive.com/hhdownloads* ***

WRITE HERE:

If you were to dare to dream your biggest dream, what would it be? Is there a million-dollar dream you once had *that you still want* to come true? Describe your million-dollar dream in detail. Include the thoughts and feelings you have about this dream.

12. YES, YOU CAN! Anything you once dreamed of, *that you still want*, you can still be, do or have. But you've got to make sure you're not stuck in old dreams.

Maybe you once wanted to backpack through Europe, get married, or open up a quiet little bookstore in the city. Do you still want any of those things?

Yes or no?

Really think about that for a minute. And then decide which is true for you.

If it's a YES as of right now, step into it. Feel the excitement of that dream again. Let the possibility of it bubble up inside of you.

And if it's a no, let the memory of it come to you and then let it continue on its way. Don't grasp at, or cling to, what's no longer yours. Dreams change, you change, and that's completely okay.

Before you do anything else, make sure that you're working with the dreams *you actually want* as of today.

Once you know what those dreams are, be like the little engine that could, and make "I know I can" your life motto.

Because yes, you can!

You can do, be and have anything that is a true dream for you as of this moment.

Not the things you once wanted—time to let all those go. And not someone else's dreams for you—those were never yours anyway. But _your_ true dreams as of right now.

Life changed you. _Connect with who you are as of this moment and update your dreams._ Make sure that what you're dreaming up is truly yours and that you actually want it.

And then go do all the things to make it happen because _YES,_ you absolutely can!

DO THIS

Below, make a list of every single thing you ever dreamed you'd do, be or have. Even the things you wanted to do when you were 4 years old (yep, even if that means you wanted to be a fairy princess, Tarzan or She-Ra the Princess of Power).

Write them all down.

Then go through that list, one by one, and _DECIDE_ which ring true for you now. Circle those.

Once you're done with that list, start a new one for the dreams that are yours right now. Write down every single thing you want or you'd love to be, do or have.

Don't worry about figuring out the details or deciding if it's actually possible. Just let yourself get back in the groove of dreaming again.

All my dreams:	My dreams right now:
....	....
....	....
....	....
....	....
....	....

WRITE HERE:

What's it feel like for you to revisit, decide about and either reignite or let go of old dreams? What's it like for you to actively decide what your dreams are as of right now?

13. WORK OUT THE DETAILS LATER. There's a misconception that you have to be 100% sure before you do something. But if you're waiting for that kind of certainty, you could be waiting for a loooooooong time.

You don't have to know it all or plan it out perfectly *before* you take action.

You don't have to have all of the answers right now. It's okay to only know some of the things. And it's okay for things to change as you go. Just *take your next best step* and keep on moving.

Set your sights on what you want and dive in. It's way too easy to think yourself out of action. If something's important to you, or you're just really curious about it, take the leap and go for it. You can work out the details later.

Uncertainty is scary. And when things don't work, it's usually not fun.

But when you get into the habit of saying "Hmmm, I think I'm going to give that a try" and then you do, the forward momentum gets going. You start to try more things and new ways. You grow that part of you that can take action and then let the pieces fall where they may.

Life starts to become more exciting. You start to become stronger and more confident.

That freedom you seek, it comes from this place. Sometimes, it works out to be amazing; other times, not so much, but at least, you tried. At least, you kept going.

There is so much power and so much strength in knowing that about yourself.

And then suddenly, something sticks. Maybe what you expected, maybe something completely new. And your life is changed forever.

DO THIS

Pick one thing you've wanted to try for a long time. *Maybe it's oysters, learning a new language or ziplining.*

Then, quickly brainstorm a list of steps to do it. Don't overthink this! Just write whatever comes to your mind.

Take the FIRST step today. **Then, come back here and check it off.**

One thing I've always wanted to try:

Quick list of steps:

WRITE HERE:

Think about the things you've been curious to try. What stopped you? Do you feel ready to take the first steps *(only first steps!)* now and see where those take you? What lets you know you're ready, or not?

....

 14. IT'S UP TO YOU. You and your life are *your* responsibility. The second you realize this and finally stop putting everyone else in the driver seat is the same second your life will be forever changed.

Yes, you have responsibilities and obligations. Yes, life doesn't always go as planned. And yes, sometimes things suck. BUT it is up to you to not let those things dictate your life.

You're here and you've got things to do. You've got a life to live. Stop wasting time!

Focus on what you <u>can</u> do. Dream a new dream. And stop giving your past and allllllll the things you see as holding you down so much freaking power!

Decide right here and now that your life is up to you.

Step into that responsibility with power and excitement. Own it all. No more excuses. No more putting other people in charge of your happiness. And no more focusing on all the stuff that's not in your control.

It's up to you to create a life you actually want to get your ass out of bed for in the mornings. And you can, the second you decide that it's actually up to you.

DO THIS

Stand in front of the mirror and make eye contact with yourself.

Put your hands over your heart and say out loud, "I take 100% ownership of me and my life. I choose to focus on what I can do and let go of what I can't. My happiness is up to me, and my time is now."

Take a deep breath and repeat!

WRITE HERE

In what ways have you been delegating responsibility that's actually yours? What are some examples of how you've been making other people responsible for things that are actually up to you? Which of these are you ready to own your part in?

••• Hint: It's really common to put other people in charge of things like setting boundaries, happiness, health and finances. It's common to repeatedly say things like "She should know better" or "He's not listening to me" or "They don't get it." When these are on repeat, it's a sign you're giving away power and responsibility that belongs to you! •••

Recap

*And suddenly, you just know it's time to start
something new and trust the magic of beginnings.*
—Meister Eckhart

I am not someone who sugarcoats things. I'm not great at faking, pretending or living in a way that I don't believe is absolutely true. And I know in my bones that if you are reading this book right now, there is still plenty of time for you.

There's plenty of time for you to dream a new dream. To reconnect with who you truly are. To get engaged. To say yes. To show up. To be happy. And to do all the things you want to do *as of this moment.*

Time goes fast. It's limited. And sometimes, the best moments feel like they're already gone. I don't know about you, but I love it here. I love my life—even the really messy parts. And I love my people. The thought of not being here with them literally makes tears well up in my eyes and my throat tighten.

*••• Remember, this took some work for me
and there are definitely times when I get caught up
regretting the time I feel like I wasted. •••*

None of us can control time. We can't get back what's already gone. Worrying about it, beating yourself up over it, being paralyzed by it—all that does is take you out of your life. It makes you miss more. It gives you more material to beat yourself up with at a later date. It does no good!

Take a deep breath, and step into the truth that *things don't last forever.* You can't run from it, avoid it or let it stop you anymore. The way I see it, life is like a big vacation. It's like this massive playground, it's THE event. It's your time to dream, to play, to go all in and to do the things you want to do because you're here now. So, why not?

Imagine yourself for a moment going on the most amazing vacation you can possibly dream of. Would you just sit in your room and be bummed out you can't be here forever? Would you focus on the parts of it that weren't going exactly as planned? Or the travel delays or detours you had to take to get here?

No. You'd get off your ass and make the most of it. You'd explore, try new things and do what *you actually want* to do! And that's exactly what you've got to do with your life.

Make the most of your moments.
Take advantage of the time you *do* have.
Of the dreams you can still dream.

Yes, it can feel scary and hard sometimes. Yes, things don't always go as planned. And yes, you don't always get exactly what you want. Sometimes, it sucks. You don't have to fix it or feel better about it. Just let it be what it is because that's just how life goes sometimes. Those moments don't define you or your life. Don't let them hijack your happiness.

Take a step back, dust yourself off and go do the next thing you can, and want, to do. Who you are and what you want matter. This is your opportunity to live like it.

Remember...

Take 5-10 minutes now to write your responses below.

My big takeaways:

Something that surprised me:

Dreams and desire(s) I reignited:

What I *can* (and want to) do now:

The 1-2 "Do This" activities I'll continue:

1.

2.

Becoming You

Undo

Decide

Reclaim

Transform

Trust

Become

Introduction

We're all different. We all have things that set us apart and make us unique. Maybe it's how you look or feel. Maybe it's the way you talk or think. Maybe it's a specific part of your history or story. Maybe it's a combination of all of the above or something completely different.

Every single one of us has a unique blueprint that makes us who we are. It's what makes you the perfect fit for just the right thing. And the trick isn't in changing who you are to become the perfect fit, it's in using what you've got so you can find the thing(s) that's just right for you.

Unfortunately, that's not the message that's often conveyed. We're taught that we have to change in order to fit in or to belong. But being different is a good thing—it's just about you being who you naturally are. And it's one of the most important steps on your path to happiness.

Trying to fit a square peg into a round hole just isn't going to work—*it's not meant to*. And you'll never find your happiness this way. I know, I tried.

I was never the cool kid, but there was a part of me that always wanted to be. I wanted to fit in and to belong, but I never really had any idea how to. I had all these things that I thought set me apart and made me different, but not in a good way. So I shoved them down and ended up getting really lost. I felt like I couldn't be me and the only way I knew how to cope at the time was with a lot of anger and a lot of rebellion.

That was pretty much my m.o. for a decade, and it led to a lot of wild times, risky behaviors and feeling out of control. Of course, the more of those experiences I had, the further from me I became. My only way to deal with it was to just keep being the person who, at my core, I actually wasn't.

It's hard to become who you are if you're always trying to deny, disown or dim down a part of you. It would be like having a left arm but refusing to acknowledge it or use it so you never ever put it through your shirt sleeve. You just leave it there, feeling it against your body, but trying to ignore it. It changes how you operate in the world.

I could feel that how I was living was in conflict with who I was, but I didn't know how to reconnect or what to do about it. I didn't know how to be me, let alone be okay with the mess I had created. And I certainly didn't know how to be vulnerable, take risks or embrace what made me unique and different. I didn't know then if I actually even wanted to!

When I was in it, I just felt really disconnected. I felt like I couldn't be myself. And I felt things like *resentment, anger and envy,* but I didn't have all this insight that I'm sharing with you now. All of that has come from my own journey of self-discovery, like the one you're on right now.

Self-discovery, growth, becoming who you are—it's an ongoing process. As humans, we're fluid beings, _always_ changing and growing. Always having experiences in life that challenge us to re-calibrate so that we are living in alignment with who we truly are.

Sometimes, it gets messy, complicated or hard, but you can handle all of that. Once you realize that it's simply a normal part of the process, it feels a lot easier to step into it. *It doesn't have anything to do* with who you are or what you're meant for—it's just the way it is.

One of the biggest lessons I've learned along the way is that *being different is a really good thing*. It lets you put your unique spin on life. In a lot of ways, it's really freeing!!! It stops you from trying so hard to be someone you're not. You worry less about what every single person thinks, and you trust more in the things that feel right to you.

I've noticed this most as a new mom and giving myself permission to do the mom thing in my own way. To know what kind of mom I want to be and to do my best to show up in that way every single day. I'm constantly checking in to see if who I am being is actually who I am or who I want to be. And reminding myself that it's okay to change things up at any point along the way.

Your differences are your thing, your unique piece to the puzzle. No one else is supposed to have it, or to understand it. And you having it means that you have a place that you fit into, one that's exactly right just for you. It means you get to live your life in your own way.

So, stop trying to fit in where you're not meant to. Stop denying parts of who you are. Don't trim your edges or change your color. Move on and find your place in this world.

Embrace *your unique combination* of traits, strengths and interests. Embrace your story and all its different parts. And express it all in how you live. That's your purpose and your path to happiness. It is the most natural, innate expression of who you are!

The information, actions and reflection prompts in this section are the how-tos of you becoming who you truly, and most naturally, are. They will lead you to shed all that armor you've been hiding under so that you can embrace your unique blueprint. This is your chance to finally be you: imperfect, messy and really truly happy. And to give yourself permission to *live your life* in your own way.

1. YOU WERE BORN BEING YOU. Your truest nature. Your temperament and traits. Your capacity for love and amazing things. They're all in there with you—and have been since the very beginning.

Even when you felt lost, disconnected or a million miles away. Even when you felt broken, scared or unsure.

You have always been there.

Life shaped you. It molded you to fit your experiences before you were able to mold your experiences to fit you.

The people, places and things that crossed your path threw you off course. Distracted you from your way. Or discouraged you from truly becoming the realist version of you.

You chose to be brave, to fit in, and to survive in a way that worked. That made sense in the moment.

Now, you're ready for a different way. You feel the part of you that's the realist you. You've heard that voice inside of you so many times before.

You're ready to listen. To finally feel like yourself *all of the time*. To be, to do and to have all the things you want. All the things you've always wanted. And to fully embrace who you've always been.

Hear your voice. Choose to listen. Trust your gut. And let *how you feel* guide every single step along the way.

DO THIS

When you're being who you truly are, everything feels exactly right. It's like the perfect fit. Everything seems to somehow just come together and go your way. And YOU feel exactly right.

Maybe you've had a glimpse here and there, or maybe you've had long periods of time when you felt this way. Tap into those times now and write them below.

Some ideas to get your mind flowing…

• Do you feel most like you in jeans and a t-shirt? Or when you wear a certain shade of lipstick? After a morning jog or a cup of coffee on the patio? Is your mind focused and task-oriented or creatively flowing?

• Did you feel most like yourself in your 30s? Or in grad school? Or when you were working on a certain project at work? Were you more connected, inspired, excited, or challenged during this time?

Then, think about what's happening in those moments. What are you doing? Who are you being? How are you feeling? What are you thinking? What are you saying? What are you wearing? Who are you with?

Tease out as many specific details as you can that describe who you're being in those moments.

Circle all of the things you can control and recreate. Bring as many as possible into your day-to-day life.

Times I feel most like me:	What I'm doing/who I'm being:
•	
•	
•	
•	

- ....
- ....
- ....

WRITE HERE

Sketch out a picture (stick figures are fine!) of you feeling and being most like yourself. Use images and words to capture as many details as possible. How often do you feel connected to this version of you? What people, places, and experiences bring out this version of you? What would have to be true in order for you to experience the real you more often, or what would you have to know, feel, think, trust or believe?

2. IT'S OKAY TO STOP PLAYING PERFECT. It's hijacking your joy, and it's totally unnecessary.

Besides, nobody really cares. You're human. You make mistakes. Welcome to the club!

The harder you try to be perfect, the harder everything else seems. And the more disconnected and alone you feel.

It's okay to be you. Exactly as you are. In all your imperfect, messy glory.

The second you let that be okay is the second everything else becomes so much easier. And it's the second you realize what's important and who your people are.

You can forget things. You can make mistakes. And you can tell the truth about it all.

Ahhhhhhh. Take a deep breath and let that sink in.

DO THIS

Think back to some of your greatest and most favorite moments in life and write those down.

Think about if they were perfect or messy. Or if they were planned or spontaneous. Think about when you laughed the easiest and the hardest. And when you felt the most genuine, real and connected.

After you list those out, think about who you're being in those moments versus who you're being when you're playing perfect, or trying hard. Write down some notes about those differences.

Which version of you is happier and enjoys life more? In what ways and why?

What would it take to bring more of that version of you into your everyday life?

What small shifts can you make right now to take the pressure off of you playing perfect and embrace your true self a little bit more?

Some of my favorite moments:

_____

_____

_____

_____

Who I was being:

_____

_____

_____

Shifts I can make:

_____

_____

_____

_____

WRITE HERE

What would open up for you if you could finally stop trying so hard to do the "right" thing and just do your thing? What feels scariest or hardest about doing things imperfectly? What are your biggest barriers to you being able to just be yourself?

....

3. SOMETIMES, YOU HAVE TO COME UNDONE. The idea of coming undone can feel really scary. It's like you're unraveling who you are.

But who you are *doesn't feel exactly right.* The roles, expectations, labels and responsibilities don't fit.

You just got into the habit of seeing yourself this way. It set you apart. Or made you feel safe. It's what has defined your identity.

But it's not *who* you actually are.

And you're ready to become a *truer* version of you.

Some, maybe even all, of the labels you've acquired, and the roles you've fulfilled, aren't the right ones for you.

Maybe you were mislabeled. Maybe you were thrown into a role you didn't actually want or that was a better fit for someone else. To get back to being who you're meant to be, you have to come undone.

You have to fall apart first.
It's the only way to really come together.

The undoing is scary. It's messy and hard because you're undoing what you've known for so long. But once all that doesn't fit is stripped away, the coming together will happen with a sense of ease. It will feel exactly right.

DO THIS

List out all the roles you fulfill and the labels you take on. For example, mom, sister, daughter, boss, peacekeeper, nice, smart, friendly, etc.

For each one, decide if it *feels right*. Imagine it like a hat—what does it look like? Maybe your daughter hat is a rainbow visor, your peacekeeper hat is a Statue of Liberty crown and your nice hat is a pink beret.

How does each one feel when you're wearing it? Imagine yourself trying it on and taking it off. And trying it on and taking it off. Then, decide which you want to keep and which you want to toss. Visualize yourself doing so.

Roles	Hats	How it feels

WRITE HERE

How did it feel to visualize and "try on" some of your different roles? How did it feel to decide about each one? Were there any that were particularly hard or easy to either keep or let go? What feels different for you now? Which hats did you decide to continue to wear? What roles did you choose to continue to fulfill? How does this feel for you now?

....

 4. YOU WRITE YOUR STORY HOWEVER YOU WANT TO. Decide about the kind of human being you want to be. Decide about who you are and how you want to show up in this world. In this life. *In your life.*

Decide. Decide. Decide.

Because you get to. You get to decide. And it's totally up to you to do so!

It's up to you to define who you are and how you act. To define your character. To decide what matters to you most. To pick your priorities and to act accordingly.

You don't owe anyone anything. You don't owe your past anything.

You get to pick and choose who and what comes into this next phase of life with you. You choose. _So, choose wisely_.

This isn't about erasing the pain or ignoring who you once were. It's about you reclaiming ownership of you and your life.

It's about you deciding what defines you. _It's about bringing who you are into how you live right now._ And it's about letting all that other stuff go.

Tune out the noise and tune in to your truth.

DO THIS

Notice the story that you tell about who you are and the life you live. For example, how do you introduce yourself? How do you answer questions like "How are you?" or "Tell me about you"? What "excuses" are you often giving or behaviors you're explaining away or rationalizing (like being late, busy or forgetful)?

Pay attention to the picture you paint of yourself, the other people and the experiences you've had.

Notice the themes in your life. For example, are you often feeling disappointed, let down or stuck? Or are people taking advantage of you or not noticing all you do?

Who are the power players? What's your role? What seems to keep happening (different versions of the same thing)? Is the story that you tell the one you want to continue?

Current story:

_____

_____

Notice if the story you tell is actually the story you want to live. Ask yourself what's working and what's not.

Are there parts of your story you'd like to change? Any themes or patterns you'd like to adjust? Anything that's working you'd like to expand or build on?

Make the updates. Tell a new story. Write it out below, in detail with specific examples. Think about what this story will look like in practice in your everyday life.

NEW/UPDATED story (the one I actually want to tell and live):

WRITE HERE

What's it feel like to write a new story? What about this story are you most excited for?

5. BE DECISIVE ABOUT YOUR LOVE. Know it. Honor it. Feel it.

It's the only way you'll ever be able to truly give it.

When you're intentional about your love, you build your life based on it. It can flow in and out freely.

But first, decide about it. Decide about who you are and what matters to you most. Decide about the kind of person you want to be. Decide about the kind of life you want to create.

Consciously decide.

Then, let those things be the guideposts for your life. Let who you are and what you stand for guide how you live and how you show up in the world.

You get to love and live how you want to. In a way that feels right. And in a way that lets you be true to who you are.

Build everything else from there.

DO THIS

Start a "who & what I love" list. Write out all the people, places and things you love. Your mom, sister or best friend. Coffee, strawberry smoothies, or pizza. Traveling, reading a book, or taking a Sunday nap.

Each day, *add at least one thing* to your list.

And each day, connect with (aka do/experience/be around) AT LEAST ONE of the things on your list.

Fill your life with who and what you love as much and as often as possible.

What matters to me most (Who & what I love):

_____

_____

_____

_____

_____

_____

WRITE HERE

What from your list are you most excited to move up on the priority list? How does it feel knowing you get to build your life around what matters to you the most (not fit it in when you can)? In what ways will your life look different when you're living it based on what matters to you the most (aka who & what you love)?

6. OWN YOUR EDGE. We all have that little bit of a wild side in us. The part of you that craves freedom. That *doesn't worry* about any of the naysaying, what ifs or about what people think. The part that just wants to let go and feel alive.

Experience life through that part of you. Feel the fun, the exhilaration and the freedom that is lying dormant inside of you right now.

So many of us have "adulted" that part out. Silenced that voice. Stuffed her down. Thinking she's too risky or irresponsible (think adolescent to 20-something self). That's she's already taken all the risks, used her 9 lives.

But she's just sitting there _waiting for you_ to let her back in the game. Sure, it's risky—but most of the really great things are.

Just imagine who you'd be if you could feel safe enough to truly be all of you. To let all parts of you in the game. The child dreamer, the 20-something risk-taker and the life-savvy adult.

That is one powerhouse trio—and it's exactly who you are!

DO THIS

Start to rock that side of you. Maybe it's with red lipstick… maybe it's with skydiving. Whatever that voice inside of you is calling you to do… give it a try!

Wear the sassy underwear. Whether that's boy shorts, granny pants, a lacy thong or nothing it all. It's whatever makes you feel like that exciting part of you.

Maybe it's different every day. But whatever it is, make sure you feel like your most beautiful, sassy self, which means anything old, dingy or just blah doesn't make the cut!

Do the shot of tequila. Dance on the bar. Dabble in the fun. Let that part of you out!

Ways I can rock my wild side/own my edge:

_____

_____

_____

_____

WRITE HERE

What are all the things that feel a little risky, sassy and fun—things that express a part of you, but you usually tame down? How does it feel to let that part of you out?

Hint: You can think about this in the context of your communication and relationships, foods you eat, music you listen to, and other lifestyle factors (i.e., saying no, speaking up, indulging in chocolate or french fries, dancing to Social Distortion, etc.). Look at all the ways you've tamed down your life.

7. EMBRACE YOUR STRENGTH AND YOUR VULNERABILITY. Yes, vulnerability is scary. A lot of times, when you feel vulnerable, you don't actually feel very strong.

You might even feel the opposite of strong. If you've ever been hurt, disappointed or let down, if you've ever failed, messed up or hurt someone you love, you may have promised yourself to *never, ever* feel that way again.

But you know what happens with all that work to protect yourself? *You actually end up <u>blocking you</u> from who you really are.*

When you vow to fend off vulnerability at all costs, you actually shut off a really important part of you. In order to reconnect with the core of who you are, you've got to flip that part back on.

It calls you to be *brave and courageous*. To risk and to trust. Which is why strength and vulnerability are part of the same. They are part of each other.

Your greatest place of power is the space where strength and vulnerability coexist inside of you.

That's where all the magic of life happens.

DO THIS

Take a few slow, deep breaths. Then, close your eyes and let yourself feel, even just for a moment, what you'd have to risk to completely be yourself, to go all in on your dreams, and to build your life from this place.

Step into it. Worst-case scenario it. Brainstorm, free-write, make it up. Just get it all—real, imagined and totally crazy—out of your head and onto this paper.

Fears, risks & worst-case scenarios:

_____

_____

_____

_____

_____

WRITE HERE

Now that you've gotten all the risks and fears out of your head and onto paper, what truly feels at greatest risk for you? Is it real? Is it true? Is it worth it?

8. YOU ARE THE HERO OF YOUR STORY. You don't need someone to come save you. You don't need someone to give you the answers. And you don't need someone to tell you where to go or what to do next.

You know you best. Stop deferring and start owning. Learn to listen to YOUR voice. Your heart. Your intuition.

Hear what YOU are saying.

Trust in the path you are on because it is the _exact right one_ for you. Feel it. Trust it. And keep moving forward, one step at a time.

That's it. That is all you have to do.

You're the one who gets to decide about you. You decide who you are, what you want and what's next. You _decide_ where you're going.

Gather your info. Filter out the noise. And keep on moving.

Trust in yourself. Once you learn to do that,
you'll never be lost again.

DO THIS

Researching, consulting and delegating are all really important skills. But before you can effectively tap into them, you need to know what _your zone of genius_ is AND what you actually want to spend your time and energy on.

Check in with yourself to explore, and really see, the who, what and when of your researching, consulting and delegating. This will help you to get a clear picture of whether you're using these resources in a helpful way, or as a crutch.

Make a list of all the experts you consult: the books, articles and websites you read, the videos you watch, the events you attend, and the people you call on for opinions. Then, get honest. Are these resources _honing or hampering_ your trust in yourself? Are they helping to make you stronger and more confident or are they acting more as a crutch?

Put a **+ for honing** or a **- for hampering** next to each one. Then, consciously decide how best to proceed with each one.

Experts, resources & consultants   **(+) or (-)**

••• Hint: _if it's honing your trust, it's probably a keeper. Look at ways to build, expand or model this relationship or resource. If it's hampering your trust or acting as a crutch in any way, it either needs to be reframed or let go—it's not doing you any favors!_ •••

WRITE HERE

If you could no longer consult with all these resources, what would you do? Are there areas of your life that you completely trust in yourself? What makes these areas different? What would have to be true in order for you to tune in and trust yourself more? What new stories or beliefs would you need to adopt?

 9. YOUR PEOPLE WILL COME. Give yourself permission to *stop trying so hard.* Let yourself be who you are. Do your thing. And don't worry so much about what anyone else has to say about it.

The right people _will show up_ at the right time when you stop trying to force the wrong people to fill in until they do.

Be patient. Trust.

And know that you don't have to fit in to belong. It's possible to be different AND still be a part of.

It's okay to embrace all of those differences and to let all the different worlds collide in a messy, beautiful and exciting way.

It's also okay to realize that some groups, people and relationships just aren't the right fit for who you are right now.

Let it all be okay. _Let yourself be brave enough to be yourself._ To step into and away from who and what you need to as you move through life.

DO THIS

In what ways are you hiding the "real you" in your relationships? For example, would you like to share your ideas at work? Be friendlier to strangers? Set boundaries with family, friends or colleagues?

What expectations or roles are you ready to break free from? How would doing this make it possible for you to show up more like yourself? What would have to be true in order for you to break free from these roles or expectations?

••• Note: _This is especially tricky with family. Childhood roles you stepped into (or were put into) can be especially challenging to break free from. They can also be the ones that build up the biggest levels of resentment._ •••

Roles and expectations I'm ready to be free from:

WRITE HERE

Imagine the freedom of being able to be yourself—no hiding, no shrinking, no pretending—just being you. Who do you think would be impacted the most and in what ways? How does that feel for you?

••• Hint: Really take a minute to think about this. Your best friend who you've been on a weight loss journey with, could she feel left behind if all of a sudden you lost the weight? Could your sister feel jealous if your career suddenly takes off? Could your partner feel threatened when you're making more money than him? Your initial reaction is going to be "No, of course not." But just consider all the potential (even if unlikely) ways in which your people may be impacted. •••

....

 10. LET YOUR JUDGMENT LEAD THE WAY. Here's the thing: every single one of us has opinions. We all have things we believe in, that we're passionate about, and that we do and don't like. We all have biases, stereotypes and preconceived notions in our brain. We just do.

It's important to know what these things are for you. Let them guide how you show up in the world. It's important to be aware of them so you know how they impact you.

You're allowed to have opinions. You're allowed to speak up for your beliefs. And you're allowed to be crystal clear on what you do AND don't like.

Yes, this is you judging. And it's perfectly okay—*just don't be an asshole*.

You're experiencing something, feeling a certain way about it and deciding if it's for you or not. That's a good thing.

It helps you sort through your values and your priorities. It's how you'll know where and when to invest your time and energy.

You get to like who and what you want. There is nothing wrong with being crystal clear about this and acting accordingly.

Just know that *you are not the only one who gets to do this*. And just because you feel a certain way doesn't mean that someone else can't feel the exact opposite.

And you'll both be exactly right—for yourselves.

So, stand strong in your judgments. And create the space for others to do the same.

When you can live like this, you create a community of people who are dynamic and intriguing. Who are willing to explore, to be challenged and to grow. That's exactly what will make your life, and the world we live in, feel vibrant and interesting.

DO THIS

Make a list of the things you feel strongly about. Maybe you love chocolate ice cream and hate fried pickles. Maybe you have strong liberal views or feel passionately connected to a conservative perspective.

Just start to get really clear on where you stand on things.

Then, challenge yourself to find someone who sees things differently from you and to learn about their view. (*They're probably a lot closer than you realize.*) ;)

Get curious, ask questions and stop yourself from chiming in with your opposite perspective. *This is not the time to convince them you're right.* Don't worry, no matter what they say, you don't have to believe it to be true.

Use this time to consider a different perspective, to hear someone's stories and to really see the person behind it all.

Engage in a new conversation. Consider the world from someone else's point of view.

You don't have to agree with a single thing they say, think or believe, but this is a great opportunity for you to expand your experience.

I know it might be hard to find someone who hates chocolate ice cream…but I imagine there are a few. ;)

Who I talked to:

_____

What we talked about:

_____

What I was most surprised to hear/see/learn:

_____

WRITE HERE

With your list of things you feel strongly about, go one by one and ask yourself, "What if I'm wrong? What if I'm wrong and fried pickles are the best thing ever?" Just play with this to see.

••• Note: Yes, I am using lighthearted examples. It's up to you to go deep! •••

The more you can expand your perspective, the better you'll be at communicating, creating and problem-solving.

....

11. YOU CAN DO HARD THINGS. Even when you think you can't, you really truly can. Becoming who you are, knowing what you want, and acting accordingly can (and will) feel hard sometimes.

But that won't matter once you realize that you can do hard things.

You can do hard things WITH EASE when what you're doing feels like a match with who you are and what you want.

Know what matters most to you and put your focus on those things. Get clear on your values. Know your priorities. Let the distractions fall away.

Don't waste time on the drama, the stories or the self-doubt.

Know that you are doing the best you can in any given moment. Even when your best is imperfect, messy or doesn't feel like it's good enough.

Just keep showing up. Keep doing your thing and do it with integrity. And keep trusting you're doing it all exactly right, regardless of how it all plays out.

DO THIS

What's one hard thing you've been putting off? Write it down below. Underneath it, write down all the steps you'll have to take to check that thing off your list.

Put the steps in order. Take the first one.

Check it off. And _then_ decide what your next step is.

••• Hint: Your next step may be on the original list of steps, it may further down the list or it may be something new you never initially even thought of! Be open to taking each step as it comes. •••

Hard thing I've been putting off:

_____

What feels hardest about it:

_____

All the steps it'll take:

_____

WRITE HERE

What if you knew that you could do every single thing you wanted or needed to do? That it might be hard but that something being hard doesn't actually mean anything about you as a person or what you're meant for. What would change? What is one thing you would do? Why that thing?

....

12. BRING YOU TO THE TABLE. You don't have to be anyone other than you—ever. You get to show up as yourself in every single area of your life.

Let the world see you. Be who you are. *Accept your mess and your imperfection.* Embrace what sets you apart and infuse it into your life.

Because what makes you different is perfect. It's what makes up your unique puzzle piece. That special combination of your natural, innate gifts that you are here to bring to life.

Embrace what that is so you can find the place where you fit in, where you belong, and where you are part of the bigger picture.

Take ownership and step into that. Get out of your own way.

And bring all of you, in full living color, out in the open for all to see.

DO THIS

Ask at least 5 people what *one word* they would use to describe you.

Person I asked: **Word:**

1.

2.

3.

4.

5.

What was this experience like for you? Does each word feel true to you? Is there anything you secretly wish others recognized about you? Were you surprised by anything?

WRITE HERE

What feels scariest about letting your people, and the world, see you—like really, truly see who you actually are?

13. DON'T SHRINK DOWN YOUR JOY. Feeling good and being happy is a good thing! Embrace it. Feel it. And let it radiate from you.

You don't have to deny all the goodness you've got going on to make other people comfortable. You don't have to shrink to let other people shine. Nope, not at all necessary.

You get to be all of you. You get to feel good. To enjoy life. To recognize, own and share all that you've got going on.

When you embrace it all, you actually become evidence for yourself *and every single person around you* for what's possible.

Your energy will be like a magnet attracting amazing things and amazing people into your life.

You don't have to shrink or dim down anything about you or your life. You shining makes our collective light brighter. It brings more goodness into the world.

It brings hope, inspiration and possibility into every corner that you let your light shine into.

So shine on.
It doesn't have to be perfect to be good!

DO THIS

Today, be the real living proof of what's possible.

Think of something you'd like to prove to be true—your "life hypothesis."

Some ideas to consider: people are mostly good, simple things brighten up the day, smiling is contagious, kindness is easy, anything is possible, you get out of life what you put into it, you can do anything you set your mind to, etc.

Then, think of one action you can take right now to prove it's true.

Life hypothesis:

_____

_____

Action I can take to prove it's true:

_____

_____

_____

WRITE HERE

In what ways have you shrunk or dimmed your light in the past? What prompted this? How will you handle these situations differently in the future?

14. YOU ARE A POWERFUL FORCE. It can be easy to forget how powerful you are. Especially when it feels like life is happening to you, and not at all for you.

Life can be hard, messy and sometimes, really unfair. It's always changing. It can be unpredictable, complicated, and it can feel really unnerving.

But that's life. It's not you. It doesn't have anything to do with who you are or what you're meant for. It doesn't define you.

You move through. You rise above. You learn. You grow. And you keep on moving.

You are not defined by the things that life throws your way. YOU DEFINE THOSE THINGS. You give them meaning. You make them matter. You do that.

You are the one who gives meaning and purpose to _your_ life.

Regardless of the hand you've been dealt, you always get to decide what to do with it.

Sometimes, it means you fold. Sometimes, it means you go all in. And sometimes, it means completely different things on different days.

Feel your purpose inside of you—written on your heart—and play your hand accordingly. Act based on what you know to be true for you. On what's inside of you, not based on what's happening outside of you or in the world around you.

And always remember that _you are_
the most powerful person in your life.

DO THIS

Bring your favorite superhero to mind. How does she/he stand right before going off to do something particularly brave or badass?

Get yourself in that stance for 5 minutes.

Strike the pose, stand there and breathe.

Feel the shift in your energy. Go do something important.

WRITE HERE

If you accepted the role as the most powerful person in your life, how would that feel? Is it a role you want? What's the scariest part about it? What's the most exciting part about it? What would you have to believe, or know is true, in order to be the most powerful person in your life?

Recap

Today, you are you, that is truer than true.
There is no one alive that is youer than you.

—Dr. Seuss

Here's what I know for sure: you matter. And who you are has *always* been with you, even if it feels hard to access. I totally get that. It was hard for me, too. For a long time, I had felt disconnected from my center. It took a lot of work (aka intentional effort) for me to get back there.

The more I changed, the more like myself I became. I started to feel, and to be, different. It was easier to live in a way that felt right, in a way that felt like me. That's available for you, too, and that's what I hope this section offered you.

I genuinely believe that every single one of us is born the truest version of who we are.

I have ultrasound photos of my son with his ankles crossed, one hand behind his head and the other hand up in the air like he's fist pumping. This is exactly how he rolls in his everyday life. He is laid back, up for anything and always having a good time. It's just who he is.

You have that innate way of being inside of you, too.

But life happened. And without even realizing it, the people, places and things you experienced early on shaped you. It doesn't mean anything bad or wrong. It doesn't mean it's anyone's fault or there's someone to blame; it's just the way it goes—it's the process of navigating this life.

It happens when you're really young. And it happens as you get older and go through different things. As you experience different phases and stages. A lot of times, you don't even really notice that anything is off; it's this gradual progression. **It's just so easy to get caught up in living and to lose track of being.**

Then, all of a sudden, things feel, or you feel, off and disconnected. It's because you've become someone other than who you are, other than who you want to be. And you're living in a way that doesn't match that truest version of you.

So, it's time to recalibrate. It's time to reconnect with yourself so you can become the truest, most natural version of who you are. You can do that. Even if at the beginning you're not sure you can.

The first step is always the hardest. But once you decide to really truly take that first step, *once you access that part of you*, it'll feel exactly right and all the other steps will happen with a sense of ease, clarity and connection—even when they're still hard.

You got this. You deserve it. You absolutely can do it. And I promise you, it's possible. I've done it and I've witnessed, coached and supported so many people on their journeys too. I've gathered so much evidence that this is possible, which is why I know it truly is possible for you, too.

Remember...

Take 5-10 minutes now to write your responses below.

My big takeaways:

Something that surprised me:

I am (words that describe you):

What I _can_ (and want to) do now:

The 1-2 "Do This" activities I'll continue:

1.

2.

3

STEP THREE

Letting Go

Let go

Heal

Forgive

Coexist

Build in

Breathe

Introduction

Do you have one of those positive, happy life phrases that drives you absolutely bat shit crazy? I do. It's any variation of "just let go."

When I hear it, it's like walking on squeaky snow or fingernails on the chalkboard (yep, two other things that drive me crazy). And there was a time (pretty much the whole 7 years of my infertility journey) when *every single time* someone said it to me, I quite literally wanted to punch them in the face.

I know, I know. That's not very coach-like, let alone human-like. But I didn't actually do it, that was just my visceral response.

What does letting go even mean? It's one of those sayings that gets thrown around a lot (even by me, sometimes). I see the value in the concept, and I get it, but it's one of those things that's so tricky and feels really counterintuitive.

This has been, by far, the hardest thing for me to wrap my head around. And I got to it when I had to face my worst-case scenario with infertility: not becoming a mom. I had to recognize that as a very real possibility, and know that I could survive (and still find a way to be happy), *WHILE AT THE SAME TIME* hold onto hope and do everything that was in my control.

It is one of the most valuable skills that any one of us will ever learn. You plan for the worst and then throw that plan out the window— basically saying, "I got it, I know what to do and it'll all be fine."

Whaaaaaat?! Yes!!! And at the exact same time, you hope for the best. Knowing and trusting and believing that however things play out *you will be okay,* maybe even more than okay.

A few years ago, one of my coaching clients was really struggling. She and her husband were trying to adopt, but two years in and not a single word. She didn't know what to do next. I had her do an exercise to help her really paint out the picture of her worst-case scenario in this situation. And to see that while this worst-case scenario would understandably suck, she could still find a way to be happy. Within a few weeks, she received a call connecting her with the birth mother of her son.

Yes, this is powerful stuff.

It's an *active* process. It's tricky because, in some ways, it feels like you're giving up. But you're not—it's about *finding peace and acceptance.* It's about finding a way to be okay with however life plays out.

Because the truth is, there is only so much that you can control. There's only so much you can do. Yes, you do all of those things, but then, that's it.

You recognize what's yours and what isn't. And you choose to make the best out of the situation because you've only got one life and you *actually want to live it.* Besides, hanging onto the past, to anger, to hurt and to resentments, to unmet expectations, to the shoulda, coulda, wouldas—none of that's going to get you anywhere anyway.

Everyone gets to this place of letting go in their own way and in their own time. There isn't a one-size-fits-all approach. It's more of a do-what-works-for-you-until-you-feel-it kind of thing.

It's that place where *you turn yourself over to life and to your faith* and you know that you'll be okay no matter what happens. It's where you literally look at the things you're most afraid of and you know that you can not only survive but thrive through them all—no matter how hard, messy or complicated it ends up being.

It's that place where you know who you are, you trust in what you're doing and you feel your way through. It's a messy, yet powerful, place to be. It's filled with waiting and trusting. With facing and choosing. With actively acting and actively loosening the vice grip on how you *think* things will go. On how you think things should go. And on how you want them to go.

I imagine it like this: you're swimming in the ocean and you get caught up in the current. Your initial reaction is to swim like crazy to get to the shore. You don't want to get pulled out to sea. You don't want to drown. *You don't want this thing that's happening to actually be happening.* And so you decide to do something that in your head seems wild and crazy. You take a deep breath, you turn over on your back and you float.

You decide to let the current take you where it's going to take you. You keep your eyes on the shoreline and you trust that you can, and will, get to where you need to go. *And you know that, in this moment, this is truly the only possible thing you can do.* You make your peace with it.

Because what you were doing—the fighting against and swimming away from—wasn't working anyway. It was doing the opposite of what you wanted it to do. So, you turn yourself over to the situation. You trust. You hope. You pray. You do all the things you know to do to give you the courage to accept, make peace with and find your way through.

This is letting go. It's the process that many of us get to when we're out of options. You just kind of throw your arms up and say "It is what it is."

Once you learn the skill, once you get the hang of it, and once you see that it's so much easier to act from this place, then it becomes the thing you do much earlier on. *It becomes the decision you make at the beginning.* Because you know that you don't want anything getting in your way or weighing you down anymore. You know that there is only so much you can do. And you know that no matter how things play out, you have the strength to handle it all.

The information, actions and reflection prompts in this section are the how-tos of letting go. They will teach you how to get unstuck, embrace life's contradictions and step into the present moment. This is your chance to finally find your freedom from all that's weighing you down and blocking your way. And to confidently step into what's next (and what's *now*) for you.

1. BREAKING UP IS HARD TO DO. The thing with change is that you have to let go of one thing to grab onto another.

Whether you're letting go of a belief, a relationship, a behavior, a goal, an old story, a piece of your history *or whatever,* there's a part of you that finds comfort and connection to that thing you're letting go.

Even when you know it has to happen. Even when you know that thing is toxic or not working for you. Even then there's a part of you that feels conflicted or sad.

That's all okay. The truth is *breaking up is hard to do.*

One of the best things that you can do is to recognize that. To let that be okay. To not fight it or beat yourself up about it.

Own it. Say "It's freaking hard." Ask for help. Talk about it. This'll make it a little bit easier, and you a whole lot stronger.

Once you feel it, you can heal it. It loses its power. You can actually move forward. And you focus on the aaaaamazingness you'll _gain_ by letting go.

DO THIS

Write one thing you want, or a goal you have. Then, list out all the things you'll have to let go of in order to get it.

For example, if you want to lose 10 lbs, you may have to let go of eating chocolate chip cookies for breakfast. Or if you want to eliminate credit card debt, you may have to stop your weekly trip to Homegoods (where you always find something you love!).

Brainstorm a list of all the things you could potentially have to let go of in order to get what you want. Go through that list and consciously DECIDE if you're willing to let each one go. Next to it, write why you're willing (or not) to do so.

My goal/want:

Let go	Willing to	why/why not

WRITE HERE

Now you have a list of things to let go. Many of those things are part of habits, traditions, comforts and likes. For each item on your list, reflect on what it means to let it go. Who will be impacted (including you!) and in what ways? How does that feel?

2. LIFE IS SHORT... Way too short to be filling it with things that are weighing you down, distracting you or hijacking your happiness.

Don't let yourself get caught up in the drama. Don't let yourself be swept away by all the things you think are "important" but really don't matter that much at all.

Shift your focus.

Let go of your need to do things "right," to not make mistakes or to make everyone else happy and comfortable.

Find your purpose, meaning and peace in the things that are right there in front of your face. Stop chasing what isn't real and what doesn't matter.

Tell a new story. Shift your perspective. *Choose to let the simple things matter more.*

See the function and the purpose in the mundane. Instead of pushing against it, step into it. See what it brings to the table.

Feel the comfort that comes from consistency and structure. Look around and see the beauty that lives in every day.

It's all right there. Life isn't calling you to "arrive." You're here— you have arrived.

Life is calling you to live. To experience. To feel, see and be.

To step into the flow of it. To be an active participant on the journey.

Let yourself see all the parts. See how it comes together. How it flows. And start to appreciate all that is already right there in front of you.

DO THIS

Take an inventory of your day. List out all that you do, from when you wake up to when you go to bed. Next to each item, put a "+" if it contributes to your overall happiness and a "-" if it takes away from it.

Make a decision about each thing—even if it seems neutral, it's not. Tally up each category. See if you have more factors that add to or take away from your overall happiness.

What, if anything, is it time to change?

Inventory of my day:

- _____
- _____
- _____
- _____
- _____
- _____

WRITE HERE

What do you see when you really slow down to look at what's right there in front of you? What have you been missing, ignoring or pushing against that you now see the value in?

3. DON'T LET YOUR PAST HIJACK YOUR FUTURE. Regardless of whether you look at your past and think of it as your "good old days" or you look back with sadness and regret—looking back too long, too much or too often will keep you from your future.

It'll stop you from being able to truly see what's out there waiting for you. And you'll miss out on all of your "good old days" that are happening *right now.*

Weave into right now what makes you smile. The pieces that help you to flow forward. And let go of what weighs you down.

All the reminders of who you once were, but no longer are. The dreams that just never came to be. All the shoulda, coulda, wouldas. And all the things that freeze you in a time that's gone—whether that's from yesterday or two decades ago—it's time to put them all where they belong—in the past.

When you do, you're giving yourself space. The space to breathe. To be present. To see what's next. *And to truly see what's possible for you as of right now.*

You have to be willing to let go of the old in order to grab onto the new.

DO THIS

Look around your home, go room by room. Do the pictures, mementos, decorations, clothes—*all of the things*—keep you connected in a way that makes you smile? Do you feel light, happy and free? OR do they weigh you down? Do you feel heavy, sad and stuck?

Are you willing to see all that's holding you back?

••• *Note: Letting go is NOT the same as forgetting.* •••

What can you use, repurpose or gift away so that your space is encouraging you to be in the current flow of your life?

_____

_____

_____

_____

_____

*** *For a room-by-room checklist, visit balancethrive.com/hhdownloads* ***

WRITE HERE

What feels scariest to you about moving forward?

 4. NOT ALL THINGS HAVE A REASON. Life happens. Random, unexpected, and sometimes, really unfair things happen.

And it's hard. Really freaking hard.

Then people say things like "Everything happens for a reason" or "It's all part of God's plan" so that we can all feel better. Like it's part of something bigger than us, therefore, we should be okay.

But it doesn't feel that way. It still feels hard, sad or unfair.

There's this part of us that wants to get it, to understand why. But then there's this other part that knows, regardless of the reason, it still sucks.

Having a reason doesn't make anything better. Knowing with our brains that something was "meant to be" or part of a "bigger purpose" doesn't do anything for our hearts.

And I believe that when we cry, God does, too.

We are here to live this life. To experience it. And to feel it.

But there are no guarantees. There's no protection from pain, loss or hardship.

Being a good person or doing the right things doesn't protect you. It's not meant to. That's the tricky part. It's up to you to live your life in a way you believe is right, while knowing that anything can happen at any time.

And that uncertainty and randomness is scary.

But you're here, on Earth—God's playground—to enjoy. To feel alive. To live as loud as you possibly can. And to help all the people around you to do the same. Because the more people who are laughing and enjoying, the better the time that's had by all.

Sometimes, people fall. Sometimes, random, shitty things happen.

It's just the way it goes. It can be hard and confusing. And that's just what it is.

That's life. You don't have to give a reason to it. Understanding doesn't heal heartache. And time just gives you distance from it.

But when you can see all this just as how it is, you learn to coexist with it.

You learn to feel it in a different way. It changes when it becomes a part of your bigger picture. When you realize that you don't have to trade the good for the bad. That somehow you can find your way with both.

Sometimes, it'll inspire you. Sometimes, you'll give purpose to it. And other times, it'll just be this random, shitty, unfair thing that happened.

When you let that be okay. When you stop trying so hard to wrap your head around something you're not actually meant to understand, that's when you'll start to find some space to heal and move forward in a new and different way.

DO THIS

Make a list of all the things in your life you've been trying to figure out why, to understand, to attach a reason to. Things that maybe you regret or wish were different. Mistakes you've made. Times you've been hurt or lost something important to you or someone you love.

Things I'm trying to figure out/understand/make sense of:

_____

_____

Go through each item and ask yourself, "Will understanding this or knowing a reason for it make a difference or help me in some way?"

If this is just one of those hard things in life, how can you let your brain off the hook—to stop replaying, trying to understand, make sense of or figure it out—and just let yourself really feel all of it, so that you can find a way to let it be. To coexist with it and to keep going.

WRITE HERE

Your head is trying to figure out/heal/understand/fix something that your heart won't ever understand. Imagine if you could let your head off the hook and just let your heart feel what it needs to. What might that be like?

5. TURN YOURSELF OVER TO THE MOMENTS THAT MATTER.
There are only so many moments that you'll have in your life.

You'll look back on the collection of all those moments some day and think to yourself, "Wow, that all went really fast."

It's going to happen like that.

You're *going* to miss things. You're *going* to forget to pay attention.

And you're going to miss this. This phase. This place in life you're in right now. Even if it's hard, there will be things about it you look back on someday *and miss*.

So when you notice you're in one of those moments that matter, turn yourself over to it. Suspend time just for a little while. Let everything slow down and just be there.

Breathe and pay attention.

Because it might be the last moment like it. You might have 100 more that you don't even notice. So don't miss this one. Let yourself *be in it* for as long as you'd like. Nothing else really matters that much.

Collect your moments whenever you can.
It's the playback reel of your life.

DO THIS

Catch yourself in the moments that matter. Whether that's playing with your pup, rocking your toddler to sleep or having a glass of wine with a friend.

It could be a moment of connection, comfort or inspiration. Whatever that moment is, be in it. Breathe it in. Pay attention to it.

Your life is a collection of *your* moments. Collect as many of the moments that matter as you possibly can.

My moments:

_____

_____

_____

_____

Keep track of these moments in a journal, scrapbook or photo album. Glue in a momento (like a valet tag, a leaf you found on a walk or the fortune out of a fortune cookie), print off and tape in a photo you snapped on your phone, or simply write down *one sentence* about it. Just a simple, quick and easy reminder is all you need.

WRITE HERE

What are some of your favorite or most memorable moments? Describe what makes these moments stand out to you.

6. SOAR IN THE IN-BETWEEN. Change is a process of holding on and of letting go. Of seeing what you want—focusing in—and going for it. Of stepping out of your comfort zone—trusting in yourself—and believing that anything truly is possible.

But there's this space, this time between where you are right now and where you want to be. This space outside of what you know but not quite yet to where you want to go. It's not usually a fun place to be in.

You feel like you're in limbo. It's uncomfortable and hard. It's easy to freak out.

You start to doubt yourself and to wonder if this new thing is meant for you. If you really _can_ do this.

You were so clear. So sure. And now you're not at all.

Think of change like that in-between flying bit a trapeze artist does when she let's go of one hand to grab for another. She soars—all in—with confidence. And maybe a little bit of fear, too.

Letting go and reaching out. Seeing and extending.

Knowing you can't hold onto the past _and_ move into the future.

Trusting in the timing. And in the preparation that led up to this moment.

Just like you. Learning to soar in the in-between.

DO THIS

Fear and excitement are on different ends of the same spectrum. It feels more like fear when all your what-ifs turn into worst-

---

case-scenario type of possibilities. So, play the what-if game. But bring BOTH sides in.

What if I fail? What if I nail it? What if I make a massive mistake? What if I make a mistake and everything's fine anyway? What if I make no mistakes?

If you're going to play the game, be willing to play it from both sides! Practice with a specific example below.

What if.....

_____

_____

_____

_____

WRITE HERE:

What would you do if you could feel all the fear and go all in on it anyway?

7. FEEL HOW YOU WANT TO FEEL. Right now. Don't wait to reach your goals or get what you want to feel the way you want to feel.

Build in the experience you want to have today. It'll help loosen your grip on what you want, on your expectations, and on how you think things should go.

It'll take the pressure off.

The new will feel much more possible. You'll feel the light at the end of your tunnel. It'll help you to be brave enough to walk into the darkness, the unknown.

It'll be the torch that guides you forward.

It'll give you a fresh perspective. It'll give you courage. And faith.

Everything will be so much easier because you're already feeling how you want to feel. All the other stuff will be a beautiful bonus to *your already* great life!

DO THIS

Create on the outside how you want to feel on the inside. Pick one word to describe how you want to feel.

Then, pick one space in your house—a room, drawer, closet, etc.—and create that feeling in the space.

For example, if you want to feel peaceful and you choose to start with your bathroom, you could paint it, bring in candles, plants or photos that inspire peace. Or if you want to feel happy and you decide to start with your closet, you could get rid of clothes that put you in a funk (because they don't fit or feel good) when you see them.

I want (space)_____to feel _____..
I'll create the feeling by:

_____

_____

_____

_____

Go through your house and ask yourself, what can I do in this space now to help me feel how I want to feel.

The more of these spaces you create, the more you'll feel how you want to feel. And the easier taking action becomes.

WRITE HERE

Go back to the one word describing how you want to feel. Does this word describe how you want to feel across all of your physical space? Or are there additional or different words for different spaces?

Note: You might want to feel light and illuminated or open and alive in all areas of your physical space (house, car, office, etc.). Or you might want to feel peaceful in your bedroom and inspired in your office. You might have a small group of 3-5 words to best describe how you want to feel.

Once you settle on your word/words, go through each space and describe in detail what this word would look like in your physical space.

Example:

Bedroom - relaxed	Office - focused	Kitchen - inspired
Neutral colors, salt lamp	Decluttered	Bright, open, organized
Lavender essential oils	Organized, green walls	Cookbooks on display
Soft bedding, blankets	Vision board, quotes	White tile, colorful artwork

How does this feel for you? In what ways can you use this information to inspire a to-do list that feels exciting (not overwhelming). *Focus on what you can do now.*

Bedroom - _____. Living Room - ____. Kitchen -_____.

 8. YOU'LL GET TO WHERE YOU WANT TO GO. Believe in that. Maybe it feels scary, hard or unclear. First steps always are. But clinging onto what was isn't helping. It's holding you back. And it's preventing you from going forward.

Going forward isn't about forgetting. It's not about denying or disowning. It's about *moving into* the next phase. It's about *stepping into* the flow of life.

And it's about bringing whatever you want and need into that phase with you.

It's also about seeing what needs to go, and letting it go.

The people, places and things that had an impact—they helped to shape you. Learn the lessons. See the value. Take an active role. And keep on going.

Bring in what you want to be a part of you, and let what you don't fall away.

Trust in the process. The flow and the movement.

You are meant to keep moving. You will get to where you want to go.

But you've got to take those steps.

The only way to find your rhythm is to keep showing up for the dance.

Go all in. Expect curveballs. Let the pieces fall where they may.

And know, above all else, that you are in the exact right place, doing the exact right thing, at the exact right time.

DO THIS

Create a mantra to help you remember that you are, in fact, showing up and doing your best. You can't control all things.

That's okay. Things don't always go as planned. But when you can trust that you are on YOUR path and that it's exactly right, it makes a world of difference.

Mantra examples:
- I trust that I'm in the exact right place, doing the exact right thing.
- I show up every day and do the best I can do.
- I'm in the process of getting to where I want to go by taking it one step at a time. I'm good with that.

My mantra:

-
-
-
-

WRITE HERE

If you completely trusted that you're in the exact right place, doing the exact right thing, and now is the exact right time—what would change? How would you do things differently from what you're doing now?

9. DON'T LEAVE ANYTHING LEFT TO WONDER ABOUT. If you're not careful, you can end up with a life full of regrets.

Things you wish you would've done. And things you wish you would've done differently.

They'll sneak up on you. And they'll snowball.

One right after the other. Piling on top of you—keeping you stuck.

Wishing things were different. Wishing you were different.

But all that wishing will get you nowhere.

So instead, decide to do things differently. Decide that starting right now, you'll do ALL THE THINGS that you wonder about.

You'll feel alive. You'll take the risks. You'll show up, say yes and dive right in.

And you'll do it without all the pressure and the drama.

Free from expectations. Free from doubt. Free from caring about how everyone else does it or who's going to have an opinion about what you do or how you do it.

Because you see that you're here to live this life. To do the things you want to do.

And to leave nothing left to regret, wish for or wonder about.

Start now. You regret much more what you didn't do, rather than what you did.

DO THIS

Create a bucket list. What are all the things you want to do in this lifetime? How do you want to feel? What do you want to see and experience? What do you wish for and wonder about?

My bucket list:

_____

_____

_____

_____

_____

_____

Circle one. List out _all_ the steps to make it happen.

Steps to make it happen:

_____

_____

_____

_____

_____

_____

_____

Circle the first step—the one you can take _today_.

WRITE HERE

What regrets do you have as of right now that you can either let go of or take action on? What do you need in order to do so?

....

 10. FOCUS ON YOUR SOLUTIONS. Anytime you're faced with a problem, acknowledge that it exists. "Yep, this is a problem."

Feel how you want to feel about it. Say what you need to say about it.

Bitch, moan, complain. And then, shift your focus.

Look for your solutions. Be diligent about finding them.

See the possibilities. Explore all the options. Ask for help.

Do what you can when you can. Let it be enough.
And keep on going.

DO THIS

Brainstorm a list of all the possible solutions (realistic or not). Let yourself play with it—get creative, make things up. Then, go through your list one by one to find **one** thing you can, and are willing to, do right now.

Do it, come back here and check it off.

Example: (Every single possible solution—realistic or not...)

Problem: Steady weight gain over past 3 years

Solutions:
- Exercise more (ugh, I hate exercise! But maybe I could find something I like—I've always wanted to try Zumba)
- Find someone who will try Zumba with me
- Stop eating dessert after every meal (maybe just one treat a day?!)
- Make desserts that I can freeze so I can enjoy one a day ;) —I'd love to be able to indulge at least a little bit!!!
- Try one of those weight loss wraps?!
- Drink more water
- Schedule a dr's appointment to see if anything else could be going on
- Find some other ways to cope with stress (walks, sitting outside with a book, etc.)
- Occupy more of my time so I'm not "bored" eating
- See if sweating it out in a sauna helps?!
- Be more mindful of what I'm eating (don't eat while working, watching tv or scrolling through Facebook)
- Try a meal delivery service
- I've seen "make your own flavored water" maybe I could try that

- Stop eating—haha, just kidding (but maybe stop snacking/ eating between meals)
- Pack my lunch instead of skipping or going through the drive thru

Problem:

Solutions:

- _____
- _____
- _____
- _____
- _____
- _____
- _____
- _____

Notice how you start to feel a stream of different ideas start to flow. This gives you a new focus for your attention and some concrete action items!

WRITE HERE

Bring to mind a current problem or sticky situation that's got you feeling a little stumped. Imagine for a moment that you actually do know the answer. How do you feel having finally figured it out? What's changed with how you now view the situation? How are you different in relation to it? What do you imagine the answer or the solution to be? If you don't know, just make it up!

II. IF YOU WANT THINGS TO BE DIFFERENT, DO THINGS DIFFERENTLY. The second you realize things aren't going the way you'd like them to, recognize it's time to do things differently.

Whether that's in your life, your inner circle, your community or the world.

You _can_ make an impact. What one person does matters.

And when you change how you show up, everyone and everything around you naturally shift, too.

Seeing something not working AND keeping things as they are pretty much guarantee things will stay exactly the same.

Getting caught up in the drama of it or feeling overwhelmed by the gravity of it isn't going to change a thing.

Change happens with action. _Get into go mode._

Let go of those unmet expectations and feelings of disappointment. Don't beat yourself up. And stop blaming everyone and everything else.

See what is. Accept that this is where you are. Decide about what's next. Move on.

Create the change in your life
that you want to see in the world.

DO THIS

Set an intention for the kind of life you want to live. Is it an inspiring one? A happy one? An adventurous one? Create a visual reminder.

For example, "My happy life." Print off a picture that sparks feelings of happiness that you can hang on your fridge or put in a frame on your desk.

Then, start to notice anything that distracts you from feeling that way. When you come in contact with the distraction, pull up the picture in your mind and ask yourself, *"What can I do right now to move through this distraction and reconnect with the intention I have for my life?"*

Do that thing.

My intention for the kind of life I want to live:

_____

_____

_____

_____

_____

WRITE HERE

What in your life would you like to see be different than what it is? What are some of the biggest distractions, deterrents, roadblocks and barriers? What can you do in response to these things?

....

12. YOU DON'T HAVE TO FIGHT SO HARD. The world isn't against you, even if it feels that way sometimes.

You've been hurt, let down and embarrassed. The people you trusted didn't do the things you needed them to do.

You've felt alone, unsure and under attack. So you shrunk down, you made yourself small so you'd be hidden. Or you came out swinging, fighting, guns blazing, feeling like it was you against the world.

It doesn't have to be this way. You don't have to hide out. You don't have to fight so hard.

Those things that have happened weren't because of you.

Some people are just shitty humans. Don't let them define who you are or how you live.

And some really good people just get caught up in their own stuff. Don't take ownership of it. It doesn't belong to you. Don't let their stuff become yours.

It's time to free yourself from that old fight. It's not you against the world.

There is way more good than bad.
And you, my friend, are part of the good.

Take a step back. Breathe. And remember: you're okay, everything is okay, you got this.

DO THIS

Think of a recent time when you were triggered into fight mode and respond to the questions.

Event:

Who and/or what was I fighting for or against?

How'd it feel?

Did it go the way I wanted it to?

What do I need to know, think and/or believe so I can stop fighting so hard?

What is one action I can take now?

WRITE HERE

What are some of the beliefs, stories, past experiences, and lessons learned you have about struggle, fairness and fighting? Is it working for you? Which of these is it time to let go or change?

....

13. FORGIVE QUICKLY. The person you're hurting the most by holding on is you.

Yes, it's easy to get caught up in what something means. In holding onto things for way too long. In believing that you're right or justified. Or that it's somehow helpful or necessary.

But choosing to truly forgive is simply *you deciding* to let something that doesn't matter anymore not matter anymore.

It doesn't make you wrong and the other person right. It doesn't mean you have to go back on anything, change where you stand or be different from who you are.

Forgiveness isn't about being okay with
—it's about moving on from.

It's about choosing to be done. It's about prioritizing your peace, your happiness and *your* life. And it's about putting things where they belong.

You get to decide when your closure happens.

Do it so you can heal. Do it so you can become whole again in a new and different way. Do it so your scars, your stories and your history fold into who you are, instead of you folding into them.

DO THIS

List out all the people, events and things that have hurt you in some way. Go one by one and say out loud, "I forgive you." Check each one off your list.

All the people, events, things, etc. that have hurt me in some way:

_____

_____

_____

_____

Remember to forgive each one _and_ to check each one off as you do!

WRITE HERE

When you forgive, what does it mean (or do you think it means) about you? Is it true?

14. BUILD YOUR OWN DAMN BRIDGE. And then walk the fuck over it.

The person who is hanging on. Who is keeping you stuck. Who is blocking you from moving forward. That person is you.

This is hard to hear. It's even harder to accept as true.

But it's important because, *in some way, you are making your life harder than it needs to be.*

Take ownership of that—look inside of you—and witness things instantly change.

DO THIS

Write down one thing that's keeping you stuck. Something that you don't like in your life. Something that feels frustrating or is an energy drain.

Then, write down ALL the ways you are contributing to it.

If you're sure you're not contributing to it in anyway, then just give yourself permission to *consider the possibility*—make something up. A great question to ask yourself is "If I were to contribute to it, what might I be doing?"

For example, a relationship with someone that is particularly hard. Think demanding in-laws, cranky neighbor, sibling you don't get along with or a challenging colleague.

What are all the ways you <u>could possibly be</u> contributing to the struggle?

Are you allowing yourself to get caught up in the drama, not setting boundaries or speaking up, spending a lot of time thinking about the issue, making it mean something about you, needing to be right, etc.?

Then, honestly decide if it's something you want to change.

Go through each of the ways you could be contributing to the situation and ask yourself, "Do I want to change this or do something differently?"

Sometimes, you just have to see that you're playing a part in it. "It takes two to tango" so you decide if you want to continue the dance or if you want to tap out.

Things keeping me stuck:

_____

_____

_____

_____

Ways I could be contributing to it, keeping it going or making it harder:

_____

_____

Is this something I want to change? If so, in what way?

WRITE HERE

What does it mean to you to consider the possibility that you are in some way responsible for or contributing to the things that aren't working in your life?

••• *Hint: For most people, this is a hard thing to wrap your head around at first, mostly because you'll have a whole lot of personal judgment about it. But this isn't about you beating yourself up—it's about you being able to see the role you play in your life, and then to make some empowered decisions about things. Know your role, see your opportunities, and do the things you can control.* •••

Recap

Holding on is believing that there's only a past;
letting go is knowing that there's a future.

—Daphne Rose Kingma

Sometimes, you end up carrying things with you in life without even realizing it. You pick them up along the way and, for whatever reason, you just never set them down. You end up holding onto things that are old and comforting, things that you once wished for, things that used to make you smile, and things that represented who you were at a different time in your life.

A lot of times you're not even really aware when the things you're holding onto go from the things that fueled you forward, that inspired you, and that brought you joy *to the things* that weighed you down.

That's why it's so important to be willing to really look at what you're holding onto, to take a step back and to see what it's actually doing for you. I held onto anger for a long, long time because I thought that it was protecting me and keeping me safe. But, in reality, it was just causing me and everyone around me a lot of pain. It was doing the opposite of what I wanted.

So, I had to choose forgiveness. And the person I had to forgive the most was me. I actually make that choice on a pretty regular basis. Anytime I'm somewhere and a memory or a thought crops up that doesn't feel good, I just immediately choose forgiveness. I say it out loud. And a funny thing happens, the memory loses its power and goes away—like when you let go of a balloon and it just flies off all zigzaggedly through the air and deflates.

Letting go is a skill. It's a decision. It's an active process. The more you practice it, the better you get at it. And the freer you'll feel.

Remember...

Take 5-10 minutes now to write your responses below.

My big takeaways:

Something that surprised me:

What I've let go:

What I can (and want to) do now:

The 1-2 "Do This" activities I'll continue:

1.

2.

4

STEP FOUR

Bringing It to Life

Choose

Feel

Step into

Adjust

Embody

Unfold

Evolve

Introduction

One of the hardest things about bringing your dreams to life is *the stories you have* around those dreams. The stories about it being too hard for you, or that *you* can't do it, or that you're not good enough. Those false stories will stop you in your tracks. *Every. Single. Time.*

The tricky thing about it, though, is that these stories are usually playing over and over again in the background of your mind, just enough below the surface so you don't even realize they're there. You set the goal to lose the weight, but you keep "self-sabotaging" with secret snacking or always meeting friends out to eat. Or you set the goal to write the book, start the business or take a big trip, but things just "keep coming up."

Life gets busy and *all the things* keep getting in the way.

It happens to me, too—all of the time. I know what I want and I know what I need to do to get there, but somehow, I get every single "reasonable" excuse that comes my way. As I've been working on wrapping up this book, I've had: a pretty big deal car issue, funky scheduling conflicts, a longer than expected house update, a kiddo with a seriously long summer cold, major writer's block and a bunch of other little random things along the way.

It's bizarre how my "best-laid plans" got thrown to the wind. And things kept getting pushed back and pushed back and pushed back! While I can't control all the things that happen all the time, I can control how I respond to the situation, *how I respond to myself* and how quickly I get back on track. That's exactly what you can control, too.

Interestingly enough, how you respond to yourself is the most important factor. If you catch yourself in the act of distraction and call yourself out in a completely non-judgmental way, you'll be quick to get yourself back on track.

Most of us can't stay focused and on track forever. A little dance between focus and distraction is normal, and to be expected. So, see it for what it is and get your butt back in gear.

But, when you catch yourself feeling stuck, distracted and taking a few too many steps in the wrong direction, push <Pause> and tease out the story that's playing in the background.

See what it is that you believe about what you deserve and what you can create. Get *all of the beliefs and stories* out of your head and onto paper so you can see in black-and-white what you're working with. (This section has a lot of strategies to help you with this). So you can *decide to shift* into a new and different story, regain your focus and get back on track.

The truth is, bringing a new dream to life can feel hard sometimes. You're learning something new and you're doing things differently than you've always done. It's not bad if something's hard; it just means you've got to take a deep breath, *grant yourself some grace and patience*, and keep on going.

It would be like changing "how" you brush your teeth or "how" you put on your pants. You're so used to doing things one way that learning to do it in a new way would take some time.

Simple things would feel hard because they're requiring your attention, your patience and a decision to do it in a new way.

You'd have to keep catching yourself in an old routine and consciously choosing to do it differently.

It's not that you can't or won't—it's that you have to keep *deciding* to persevere until you get it, and it sticks.

Remember: none of this is a big deal. It's all to be expected. It's all part of the process. And it's all fine! There is always a learning curve when you're doing something new. It doesn't mean anything more than that!

You're not supposed to know how to do it all the right way at the beginning. *You're not supposed to get it without ever making mistakes.* It's meant to challenge you, to surprise you and to push you outside of your comfort zone because *you are bringing something new to life*!

If it challenges you, you know you're doing it exactly right!

The information, actions and reflection prompts in this section are the how-tos of creating and bringing something new to life. They will lead you to set intentions, make decisions and take action. This is your chance to step powerfully into your role of creator and life magic-maker. And to see, trust and believe in all that's possible for you!

1. CHOOSE YOUR YES WISELY. Know what you're saying yes to *at all times*. Know what you are allowing in, what you're making room for and what you're saying is okay. And know what you're blocking, ignoring, denying and keeping out.

You are always saying yes to something. Take an active role in that yes. Make sure the things you're saying yes to are the things you actually want to be saying yes to.
Make sure that how you're living is a true representation of who you are and what you want.

Taking action on your dreams is about you bringing a new, truer version of you to life. It's about embodying all the things that make up the core of who you are—of who you want to become—and radiating those things out into every single area of your life.

Take full responsibility for every single thing you're saying yes to.

Take ownership of who you are being in every moment. And make sure that who you are being and how you are living represent exactly what you want them to.

DO THIS

Catch your yeses today. Set a timer on your phone to go off every hour. When it goes off, pause what you're doing and ask yourself "What am I saying yes to right now?"

Are you saying yes to zoning out on social media? To getting caught up in office drama? To a second doughnut 'because it's free' at the office? To ice cream, chips, popcorn or some other snack on the couch for dinner?

And then ask yourself, "Is this yes a match for who I am or who I want to become and what I say I want?"

Start to become aware of what exactly you're saying yes to, and if it's the kind of yes you actually want.

My yeses today:

_____

_____

_____

WRITE HERE

What are you saying yes to that you're most surprised about? What about it feels surprising? What changes in your yeses are you ready to make?

2. NEVER UNDERESTIMATE THE POWER OF MAKING A DECISION. When you decide, everything changes to get on board with that choice. Your mindset, beliefs and actions move to match what you've decided about.

The power is in making the choice
—*that* is the point when everything changes.

The outcome matters, but not as much. Because by the time you get there, you're different. You see what you can do and who you can become, even if it's not exactly as you had imagined.

The decision is what inspires all the change. It propels you forward and moves you to step into what's next. It's *all about* the decision.

Decide on who you want to be. Decide on the kind of life you want to live. And then, decide to go do all the things to bring that version of you to life.

DO THIS

Today, catch yourself saying things like "Whatever," or "I don't care" or "It's up to you." When you do, *decide* to instead give a clear, concrete and honest opinion.

Decisions I made today:

_____

_____

_____

_____

WRITE HERE

Did it feel comfortable for you to make decisions? What's your perspective on and opinion about decisive people? What do you worry about or what feels most bothersome to you about being so clearly decisive (i.e., being seen as bossy, abrupt, inconsiderate, a bitch, opinionated, selfish, etc.)? What needs to change so you feel confident about being decisive *and voicing* those decisions?

3. SET THE INTENTION. TAKE THE ACTION. LET GO OF THE REST. It's so easy to get caught up in the thinking. And the planning. And the controlling. To get fixated on the outcome. On how you think things "should" go.

But you know what happens when you do this??? You start to hold on too tight. You suffocate all the possibility out. You block all the things that could be, but that you never even considered.

And then things don't work out. And you start to get scared. So you try to control and plan and think more. Only to get more stuck. And more afraid.

Your action ends up coming from a place of avoiding. From avoiding your fears. And your worst-case scenarios.

You get so fixated on avoiding that you block yourself from creating. From becoming. From moving forward.

But guess what?! There's only so much you can do. You can't control all things. You can't account for all the factors. Life just doesn't work that way.

You can do every single thing "right" and still not have things work out the way you thought they would. *Things don't always go according to plan.*

I know. Annoying, right?!

But that doesn't mean that they're bad or wrong or not good enough. When you can set the intention/the goal/the focus… and take the next best step… and then go from there, you open yourself up to all the possibilities.

You trust in your path. You step into the flow of life. You control what you can. You let go of the rest. And you don't give meaning to every single thing.

You realize every single thing doesn't have to mean something big. Sometimes, life just happens. It's just the ways things go.

And when you can step into that mindset, you stop triggering your fears. You stop making everything mean something about you. And you stop trying to control it all.

You worry less about your plan, and you let it all be okay. You take the steps, one at a time, and you see where each one takes you. You repeat the process. Set the intention. Take the action. Let go of the rest.

Step into this flow. Let the details unfold. And watch as the magic of your life happens.

DO THIS

Set an intention for how you want to feel today.

Take 2 minutes to brainstorm a quick list of actions you can take to feel that way.

Pick one and take it. Check each one off as you go.

Repeat this process 3-5 times throughout your day.

Example: Today I want to feel: Happy

Actions I can take:

- Drink water first thing (always makes me feel good to know I'm doing something healthy for my body)
- Do 5 minutes of stretches (feels so good after I wake up!)
- Skip checking my phone in the morning
- Eat breakfast (I LOVE strawberry smoothies and the bright color always makes me smile)
- Leave 5 minutes early so I feel relaxed on my drive
- Listen to music that makes me feel upbeat in the car or something uplifting or inspiring
- Bring my coffee so I don't get caught up in work gossip first thing in the morning
- Sit outside for lunch
- Smile
- Meet Kathy for a "happy hour" lake walk
- Go to bed reflecting on what I'm grateful for from the day

Today I want to feel: _____

Actions I can take to feel that way:

- _____
- _____
- _____
- _____
- _____

-
-
-

••• Notice how the actions that come to you change based on your energy, mood, mindset, environment and set of circumstances. Practicing this throughout your day helps you to see and understand how it's all connected on a larger scale.•••

WRITE HERE

Are you a planner by nature? In what ways does planning feel most helpful to you? What feels most challenging to you about letting the details unfold as you go? Do you see a way to find some balance between "planning" and "going with the flow"?

4. LET YOUR VISION LEAD YOU. Get crystal clear on exactly what it is you want.

And then open yourself up to all the possibilities. Play with your vision. Imagine. Dream. Feel into the energy of it. Embody it.

Change out the details. Let things come and go. Always trust in what you get. This is the stuff miracles are made of. You dream the dream. You take the steps and you see what life brings your way.

You let your vision lead you. You show up for the dance. And you find your rhythm.

> You say yes to doing the things you can.
> And you find peace with the things you can't.

Become the evidence that anything is possible. That miracles happen every day.

And that dreams really do come true.

You become that evidence by dreaming, by believing and by doing. Don't stop.

DO THIS

Think about all the things you hope are true. Here are some ideas to get you started: *most people are mostly good, kindness matters, one person can make a difference, etc.*

Then <u>pick one</u> you feel most strongly about. Brainstorm a list of all the ways **you** can prove that to be true. Think about how you can be the evidence of this truth.

Today, do the things on your list.

See what's it's like to *intentionally live your truth and be the evidence* for what you believe in.

I believe:

Ways I can prove it true:

WRITE HERE

Your actions are the examples of "how to live" your belief. *You are proving what you believe to be true by the actions you take every single day.* So, if you believe people are mostly good, odds are, you act in such a way that you believe a person who is mostly good does. Maybe you hold the door open for people or you say "please" and "thank you." Maybe you smile at strangers or do weekly volunteer work. You are your belief in action. You are the evidence for what you believe.

How does it feel knowing that the actions you take every single day can be the evidence for someone else about what's true or possible?

5. CONFIDENCE COMES FROM ACTION. It's okay to not know everything first. To not cross all your t's or dot all your i's before taking your first step.

Acting before perfecting is NOT irresponsible.

It's normal to feel like you don't know enough before you begin. And there's always going to be more for you to learn, to know and to do.

Things are constantly evolving.

And it's way too easy to become paralyzed in preparing. To get stuck making sure everything's "right" first. To get distracted away from action.

But things will naturally unfold as you go.

The best and fastest way forward comes from taking the steps—one at a time. From seeing how it goes. From learning what you need to learn. And then, from moving forward.

It's okay to fail, to mess up and to make mistakes. Just fail fast and fail forward. See what works for you and what doesn't so you can act accordingly next time.

And watch as your confidence grows no matter what happens... *but especially after* you survive shit hitting the fan.

DO THIS

Pick one thing you want to do but aren't quite yet "ready" to do.

Write it here:

Write your "do it date" here:

Go schedule it on your calendar.

Give yourself the chance to prepare what you need to, but *make that date non-negotiable.* Do the thing on the date, as scheduled!

Come back here and check it off when it's done.

WRITE HERE

Think of something you'd like to do, but know only a little bit about. Write out all you think you need to know before you can actually make it happen. Review what you wrote. Are these things you *actually need to know* or do before you begin?

6. IT TAKES BOLD STEPS TO BRING NEW DREAMS TO LIFE. The steps don't have to be pretty or perfect, but they do have to be bold. They have to be focused forward. And you have to be willing to take them *even though* you're not sure about the outcome.

First steps ALWAYS feel the hardest.

Know what you want. *Be crystal clear about your vision.* And then take the steps. The bold, brave, scary steps forward. Into the unknown. And into what's next.

Get into the momentum of movement. Step into the flow of action. And be open to however things play out.

Take what you get. Recalibrate. Do what you need to do. And then take another step. And then do it again.

Keep taking the bold, focused forward steps. And keep recalibrating along the way.

Be focused AND flexible.

And be amazed as you bring dreams you never even knew you had to life!

DO THIS

Pick ONE goal. Then list out all the **first steps** you could possibly take.

My goal:

All the potential FIRST steps:

Circle one that you're willing, ready and able to take today.

Take that one step. Come back here and check it off. Repeat.

WRITE HERE

What about your dreams actually coming true feels the scariest?

7. YOU WILL FALL DOWN. And you *can* get back up. When you go all in on life, you will get your ass kicked. You will fall on your face. You will feel uncertain and unsteady and wonder what the actual fuck you're doing.

But you'll also feel alive. And excited. And inspired.

And you'll know that you're on the right path. That you're getting closer to where you want to be.

And you'll keep going, even when it seems like the craziest thing ever to do. Because you also know it's the exact right thing *for you* to do.

You won't listen to "logic" because that voice inside of you knows better *even when* it doesn't make any sense.

You won't care what anyone else has to say because what you're doing, while hard, *feels exactly right.*

And you won't stop taking the steps, making the adjustments, or doing all the things you need to do. Because you know you're doing what you need to do to get you to where you want to go. You can get back up no matter what's thrown your way. Life happens. And you can handle it.

Don't ever let falling down become a bigger deal than getting back up.

DO THIS

Make a list of all the things you currently know how to do that you had to learn. Bring it back to the very basics: *walking, drinking out of a cup, talking, using silverware, catching a ball, getting dressed, brushing your teeth, counting, etc.*

The list of all the things you do, every single day, without even thinking about it is LONG.

Give yourself a reality check about the time it took you to learn how to do the things that you now just do very naturally.

Things I've learned in my lifetime...

_____

_____

_____

_____

_____

_____

_____

_____

As a bonus, spend some time with a baby or toddler who is learning how to do these things. Watch as he fails a million times, yet keeps on going, determined to learn the new skill. THIS WAS YOU, TOO!

WRITE HERE

What does falling (aka failing, messing up, not reaching your goal, etc.) mean to, and about, you? Is it true?

8. FEEL THE FEAR, AND DO IT ANYWAY. It's okay to be afraid. Fear is not a bad thing. It's just one of the feelings in the wide range of feelings we humans feel. (It also happens to fall on the same spectrum as excitement.)

When you stop being afraid of fear, fear stops making the decisions for you.

You can feel the fear and do it anyway. When you realize this, the impossible becomes possible. There are no more limits. You get to do all the things you actually want to do.

The problem with fear is when there's resistance to it.

Imagine feeling it and instead of avoiding it or fighting against it, thinking "Oh hey there, fear. I know you. What's up? Got something important to share or are you just showing up to make sure I'm safe? Thanks for that. I know I'm a little freaked out right now, but I got this. I'm okay. Peace out."
And then you do the damn thing.

Fear shows up with a lot of valuable information. It's an important emotion. And when you learn to feel it, to tune in to it and to then actively decide what to do next, it gives you your power back.

You don't have to *not* be afraid. But you do need to not be afraid to be afraid.

Feel it. Listen to it. Hear what it's trying to say to you.

And then, go do the things you actually want to do.

DO THIS

Think of <u>ONE</u> thing you're afraid of but, at the same time, curious about or kind of want to do. Some ideas: *start an online dating profile, try rock climbing, see a movie solo, try out a new class at the gym, learn to swim, take a college course, go snorkeling, publish a short story, start a blog, go backpacking—whatever.*

Then, make a list of all the reasons <u>not</u> to do it. What is your fear telling you? Look at those reasons: are they more valid, important, or relevant than your reasons <u>to</u> do it?

Circle yes or no.

P.S. Whatever your answer here is fine. The goal is to gather the information that your fear is trying to make you aware of and to make a calm, conscious decision *(that feels good)* about what to do next. That's it.

Scary thing I kind of want to do:

My reasons not to do it:

WRITE HERE

What is your fear telling you? Is it right/accurate/true?

9. DO MORE OF WHAT YOU LOVE AND LESS OF WHAT YOU DON'T. You are meant to enjoy your life. You've been given a certain set of skills, strengths and interests—that combination is unique to you and you alone.

Dive into those things. Nerd out on every single aspect. Bring them to life *in your life.*

Do what you love to do.

If you love to fish, fish. If you love to read, read. If you love to travel, travel. *It really is that simple.*

When you give yourself permission to do the things you actually want to do, you'll start to see new and different ways to do those things. You'll start to find solutions to all the barriers you're so used to throwing down (no time, other things to focus on, my people need me).

You'll find ways to dip your toes in and to really enjoy what you love again.

It starts with you *giving yourself permission* to do more of what you love. And to start saying no to all that stuff that feels like it's sucking the life out of you.

Yes, you have obligations—stuff you just have to do. BUT those things won't be such a big deal once you're doing more of what you love. You'll see the purpose and function in those things. And they'll just become less relevant to you.

DO THIS

Make a list of your favorite things to do, even if they seem silly, selfish or you have absolutely no time for them. Each day, pick one and ask yourself "What could I do today, even for just 15 minutes, that would let me experience this thing I love?"

If you love to travel, you won't be able to fly to Italy and back in 15 minutes (unless, of course, you have some kind of time machine) but you could start planning a trip, cook up some pasta or listen to a "how to speak Italian" audiobook. These are all ways to bring what you love into your life *right now.*

I love to:

_____

_____

_____

_____

WRITE HERE

How does it *honestly* feel for you to think about doing more of what you love? What are some of the thoughts, stories and beliefs that pop up? Are they true?

10. LET IT BE EASY. There are so many little things in life that can quickly turn into big things. And when that happens, life feels hard. Like really, really hard.

Not in the good "let me rise to the challenge" kind of way, but in the "what am I doing/I don't know how/I can't do this" kind of way.

So, you look outside of yourself for answers. Only to end up comparing, overthinking or getting caught up in all the drama. Ultimately getting more stuck—feeling like you're running your ass off in quicksand.

There's this question you can ask yourself that'll change everything.

One that, at first glance, you might resist because you can't even begin to see how it could be helpful or true.

But then, you'll sit with it for awhile. You'll let the defensiveness fall away. And you'll consider the possibility that it could help.

That things might be able to be just a little bit easier. And that the answers actually lie within you.

With this new perspective, everything will change.

Ready for that question?

Make sure you're an absolute yes before you read it.

Take a deep breath.

And consider this: in what ways am I making things harder for me?

It's okay if your first reaction is a defensive one (it was for me, too).

But it is one of the fastest ways to turn things around, reach your goals, and create the life you want. In a way that feels so much easier than it does right now.

DO THIS

Throughout your day, start to ask yourself, "What can I do to let this feel easier?"

Maybe it's taking some deep breaths, setting boundaries, asserting yourself, asking for help, going for a walk, delegating, taking a timeout, letting go of control, letting go of a belief or of doing it in a certain way. Maybe it's something else entirely.

Just ask yourself the question and see what comes to you.

And then start doing those things. These are your "easy buttons." Start to keep track of all the ways you could let things be even just a tiny bit easier.

My list of easy buttons:

WRITE HERE

Find your easy button. Look at all the things in your life that feel hard. What's your role in those things? In what ways might you be making them harder than they need to be? Do you want them to feel easier? Why or why not?

....

 II. DON'T LET YOUR EXPECTATIONS LIMIT YOU. Things don't always go as planned. You won't always get what you want. But that's okay.

As long as you keep making adjustments. And as long as you keep moving forward, *you will live a great life.* You will find you purpose, your meaning and your happiness.

You will reach your goals and do amazing things.

The key is to be open to things coming together *differently* from what you had planned. To trust that you're on the exact right path, even if it looks different from what you had imagined. And to know that life isn't linear, it's not always fair, but that doesn't mean anything about who you are or what you deserve.

Life happens. You're thrown curveballs. Your great ideas and best-laid plans crumble to pieces. But when you keep on moving, you open yourself up to new, better and different. Oftentimes, things you never could have dreamed up before.

So don't limit yourself by your expectations. Don't put yourself in a box with how you think things "should" go. And don't get weighed down with disappointments.

Recalibrate, consider different possibilities and dream new dreams. Play with the details—give yourself permission to adjust, let go and keep going.

Focus on how you want to feel and do the things
you can to feel that way in this moment,
even when the details are different
from when you began.

DO THIS

Write down one word to describe how you want to feel here:_____. Then, identify ONE thing you can do right now to feel that way.

For example, if you want to feel happy, you could look at a picture that makes you smile. If you want to feel calm, you could take 3 slow deep breaths. If you want to feel inspired, you could go for a walk outside. If you want to feel connected, you could call your sister. If you want to feel focused, you could turn off your wifi.

Go do that one thing right now.

WRITE HERE

The more you hold onto the way you think things should go (or should have gone), the more disappointed and stuck you'll feel. Spend the next 15 minutes free-writing your expectations about the goals/ dreams/ intentions you're trying to bring to life and what it would be like to let them all go.

....

12. YOU REGRET MOST WHAT YOU DON'T DO. So, take the risk. Do the things. ALL OF THE THINGS.

Because in the end, if it all works out, *you'll be so freaking glad you did it.* AND if in the end, it doesn't work out, you'll STILL be *so freaking glad that you tried!!!*

That you showed up. Said yes. Gave it your all. And did EVERY SINGLE THING you could possibly do.

That's the stuff you'll be proud of. That's the stuff that actually matters. And that's the stuff that courage and confidence and success comes from: laying it all on the line, showing up and doing the damn thing.

You got this. Now, go get it! ;)

DO THIS

Write down one thing/event/experience you regret.

What about it do you regret? If given the opportunity again, what would you do differently?

Those "things you'd do differently" are your lessons learned.

Pick one current situation to which you can apply one of those lessons.

Then, come back here and write down how it went.

Thing I regret:

Lessons I learned:

Current situation & how it went:

WRITE HERE

Fast-forward five years, what current-day situations have the potential to turn into things you'll regret if you don't start to do things differently?

....

 13. IF, AT FIRST, YOU DON'T SUCCEED—DECIDE, TRY AND GO AGAIN. Stepping outside of your comfort zone is scary and it's supposed to be. You're outside of what feels comfortable to you. That's the whole point.

But don't let that discomfort be the deciding factor about what's for you and what's not!

The first time for anything is always the scariest. Your perspective, thoughts, beliefs and behaviors will be skewed by how this new, uncomfortable and different experience feels.

You'll be unsure of your footing. Your senses will be heightened. And you'll be learning as you go.

Expect all of this—it's normal. So, if that first time around, you fall down or freak out. If you don't like it, love it or want more of it. If you mostly hate it and are thinking "Fuck this" the entire time, that's okay.

Get it done. Take some time, let all the dust settle and then go again.

A great philosophy for life is to try (most) things twice.

The second time clarifies *how you really feel* about something. And then you can know, with much more certainty, if something's for you or not.

DO THIS

Try something new. Maybe it's snorkeling, oysters or skydiving. Gather enough courage and go for it. No matter how it goes, give it another try. *And then* decide if it's for you or not.

My "try it twice" list:

_____

_____

_____

_____

_____

WRITE HERE

What's something you tried one time in the past and decided it wasn't for you? What thoughts and feelings let you know this? Do you think it'd be any different if you tried again? Are you willing to try it again to find out?

....

 14. GIVE YOURSELF THE CHANCE TO SEE WHO YOU CAN BECOME. And you are *the only one* who can do that.

It's up to you to dream your dreams.
To believe in yourself. And to do all the things
you can to make it happen.

It's up to you to take the steps. It's up to you to trust. And it's up to you to get up no matter how many times you fall.

You are the only one who can hear the true sound of your heart. Listen in and act accordingly. Even if it feels scary, sometimes. Even if it feels hard or overwhelming. And even if you don't always know exactly what you're doing.

It's all okay. Because you know you. You know who you are and what you want. And when you come from that place—when you create your life from there—you can't go wrong!

Even if mistakes happen. Even if you get lost on a detour. And even if things don't go as planned.

Keep showing up for yourself. Keep taking the action. And keep doing all the things. You will get somewhere amazing.

And you'll laugh more and live louder than you ever thought was possible. Because your life will be this amazing, beautiful, messy and true expression of exactly who you are.

Trust in yourself.

Take the steps.

Show up.

Go all in.

Give it your all because you will get out of things what you put into them. And you deserve to get some truly amazing things out of your life.

Always be up for anything and chase your dreams with all you've got!

DO THIS

In the middle of the page on page 177, write your name. And then in mind-mapping style, brainstorm all the things that would exist in your life if you deserved to have all the amazing things show up in your life.

Get creative: doodle, write, draw, and cut out images and words from magazines. Think about all the different categories of your life: health, career, money, relationships, community, etc.

Example on next page:

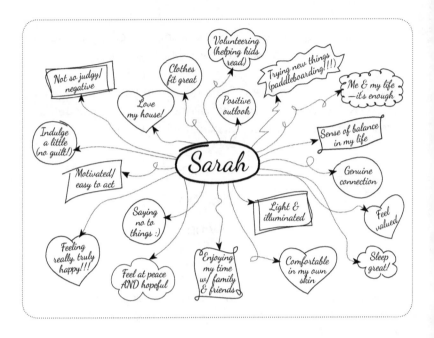

WRITE HERE

Do you believe you deserve to live an amazing life? Why or why not?

Recap

What you get by achieving your goals is not as important as what you become by achieving your goals.

—Zig Ziglar

I have this unique perspective happening right now: I work with people on developing new habits and routines, while also being a mom of a toddler who is learning everything for the first time.

It's fascinating to me to see how a person operates before having all those b.s. stories in their head. It's a reminder to me about how we operate innately in this world, and it inspires me to bring that to my clients.

I've watched my son learn how to do every single thing he can currently do. I've watched him learn to roll over and to crawl. I've watched him learn to walk and to run. I've watched him learn to talk, to eat with a spoon, to drink out of a cup, to climb up and down the stairs, to brush his teeth and to do so, so many other things. And I've watched him try and fail and try and fail and try and fail until he finally gets it.

He keeps getting back up. He keeps trying again. He keeps going until he does it. That's also how you learned how to do all those things I listed above and so much more, too.

But somewhere along the line, you stopped trusting in your ability to keep trying, and in your ability to actually do the things you want to do. Let this section remind you that you can, and are meant to, create a truly amazing life. You are absolutely capable of doing the things to make it happen—you always have been, and always will be.

It's up to you.
And yes, you absolutely can.

Remember...

Take 5-10 minutes now to write your responses below.

My big takeaways:

Something that surprised me:

I'm saying yes to:

What I _can_ (and want to) do now:

The 1-2 "Do This" activities I'll continue:

1.

2.

5

STEP FIVE

Being Happy Anyway

Imperfect

Messy

Deserving

Worthy

Happy

Introduction

I am a woman, a wife and a mom. I'm an entrepreneur, a coach and a writer. I have all the things I once wanted and now that I'm here, I want more!!!

That's the funny thing with life and dreams and wanting things. *You get to that new place and you start thinking about what's next.* It's not at all that you don't appreciate what you have, it's just that *life is always pulling us forward,* calling us to what's next.

Each one of us has to find our own way to do that little dance between being present and appreciating what you have WHILE ALSO going for more and stepping towards what's next.

When you can find some form of "balance" between the two (*which, by the way, is not the traditional meaning of balance*), it's a really amazing place to be in. My life feels messy and complicated, sometimes even hard. I make mistakes and I do things imperfectly. And things somehow rarely ever go according to plan. (*I'm always driving my hubby crazy with my "plans" and how I underestimate the time it'll take to do the things I want to do. I'm usually off by at least an hour…or two…sometimes, days.*)

BUT my life also feels really happy, interesting and full. I feel *confident in who I am* and connected to the people I love. The things I'm doing right now feel like the "right" things, even if I don't always know "how" to do them. And it's easier for me to tap back into that sense of trust and ease within me, regardless of what's going on around me.

That does _not_ mean my life is without challenges.

Money, marriage, parenting, health, relationships… Each one of these categories has challenged me at some point, forced me to take a step back, and to question what I want, who I am being _and if that's actually who I am and who I want to be._ And even though that has felt really hard at times, it doesn't completely take over, paralyze me or infiltrate all the other areas of my life (like infertility once did).

One situation, struggle, challenge or event doesn't take away from, or define, me or my life. Just like it _doesn't define you_ either. But you have to learn how to live in the mess _and_ in the imperfection _and_ in the hard stuff, to deal with it as you need to, and to put it where it belongs so it doesn't consume you.

Life is full of contradictions, and nothing lasts forever, which is why you've got to learn how to get comfortable with the natural, and messy, ebb and flow of it all! Because that's also where you find a lot of the beauty and the good.

It's all mashed up together.

It helps to _get crystal clear on your priorities,_ and to put them in an order that makes sense to you. When I became a mom, I completely turned myself over to it. It became my everything _and it was awesome._ But as life kept going, I started to realize that being a mom first and putting everything else after that wasn't actually working. While being a mom felt like my most important role, I started to see that being a woman and a wife needed to come first. They were like the rivers that fed the ocean, not the other way around. I am a better (more attentive and happier) mom when I pay more attention to who I am as a woman and a wife.

I also know that my priorities as a mom are simply that my kid knows he is loved and that we laugh at least once during the day. These are really easy things to focus on, and it makes it really easy to let a lot of other stuff go.

Knowing what matters to you most is a game-changer—it's what filters your perspective and helps you to not get caught up in the day-to-day stress and drama of life (well, at least most of the time).

Life can be messy and complicated sometimes. While you are amazing, you're also human, which means you're imperfect and you make mistakes. But when you can stay grounded in who you are and what matters to you most, you become like a ship perfectly navigating the sea—no matter how choppy the waters.

The information, actions and reflection prompts in this section are the how-tos of being happy anyway. They'll help you to redefine balance, and to see that it's not too late. Happiness happens even when life is messy, complicated or hard. This is your chance to be the real, true version of you—imperfect _and_ amazing. And to finally see that anything is possible. Miracles happen every single day and they can (have and will) happen for you, too!

1. HAPPINESS IS LIVING AN IMPERFECT LIFE AND ENJOYING IT ANYWAY. Here's the deal: life is messy, imperfect, and really freaking hard sometimes. But you can still find a way to enjoy it.

It's not about finding the silver lining in all things. *You don't have to Polyanna your way through life,* but you do have to be okay with who you are and how you're living. You've got to know that you're showing up and doing your best. And that when things don't work out or go as planned, *when things get messy (because they will), it's just life.* Tough breaks and not-so-great things don't actually mean anything about you.

The bad doesn't have to hijack the good. They can (and do) co-exist just fine. We just don't always see it. *The good, the happiness—it's all around you, right at your fingertips. It's the simple things you've forgotten to notice as life got messy, imperfect or hard.* It's all the stuff you see, hear and feel when you slow down and pay attention.

So yes, you can still be happy. You can still appreciate a beautiful sunset or the full moon lighting up the night sky. You can still laugh trying to catch lightning bugs like you once did as a kid or while running along the beach with your dog. You can still have important conversations over a glass of wine with a friend or laugh while cooking up a favorite recipe with your mom.

You can do all of these things and so much more *even when life isn't really going your way.* Even when things are messy, imperfect or really freaking hard. You can do this because you know it's just life. It ebbs and it flows. It's simply the way it goes. There are no guarantees. But it doesn't have to hijack your happiness.

So you show up, do your thing,
and make the best of the moments you've got.

That's all any of us can do. And you do it by focusing more on the little stuff which is actually the big stuff—the stuff that matters most.

You do it by remembering what's always made you smile. And by letting all the good, the bad and everything in between _collide_ _into each other_ because that's just what happens in life. It's one big beautiful mess.

And you do it by trusting that in all of the moments, you can find the part that's beautiful even when it's hidden deep within the mess. Your happiness is really about stringing together as many happy moments as you can.

DO THIS

Create a list of "simple things" that bring a smile to your face, make you laugh or brighten up your day. Today, snap a photo of you with one of those "simple things." And from this day forward, find one (or more) of those things to experience _every single day_ AND find one more to add to your list. Think of simple, readily accessible things. It'll make it easier to do more of them during the day.

Some examples to get you thinking: walking barefoot in the grass, seeing a butterfly flutter by, playing with your dog, going for a walk in the park, meeting a friend for coffee, sitting on a porch swing, looking at old photos that make you smile, drinking lemonade on a hot summer day, going for a wolk in the snow, being with someone you love, and finishing the crossword.

Simple things that make me smile or brighten up my day:

WRITE HERE

In what ways has your happiness become overly complicated or dependent on "big deal" things? Are you ready to shift that?

....

 2. BALANCE IS MESSY. It's imperfect. It's a moment-to-moment kind of thing. It requires clarity, decisiveness and a *willingness to say no and to set boundaries.*

It's not about doing all of the things all of the time. It's not about juggling all the balls all at once and never dropping a single one. It's not about all things being perfect or keeping it all together. Nope, that's not it at all!!!

Balance is a constant give-and-take. It's moments of peace and calm sprinkled with a dash of crazy. It's dropping the ball (or all of the balls) sometimes. And every so often, it's about just saying "Fuck it all!!!"

It's about knowing that some days will be better than others and being okay with all of it. It's about a willingness to make mistakes and to re-evaluate as you go. It's about *showing up every single day at your best*—whether that's you being on point or a total hot mess. It's about letting it be what it is while also doing what you can.

187

Balance is about knowing what matters to you most and choosing to spend your time accordingly. It's about *focusing on your priorities*. It's about saying no to things. It's about not feeling the pressure to do, be or have all of the things all of the time, but instead, having the most important things most of the time.

And it's about letting you, and your life, be enough exactly as is.

DO THIS

Write down your top 3 priorities <u>*at this stage in your life*</u>. Then, mentally survey your day-to-day activities to see if they're a match for those priorities. Note how much time you spend each day living/doing/experiencing what matters to you most, and how much time you spend distracted from it.

My top 3 priorities: **Activities & Time**

1.

2.

3.

Take this one step further: track the amount of time you spend on your computer or phone in a day. Set a timer every time you hop on so you can see how many minutes (probably hours) you're actually spending online. It'll surprise you. Notice how much more time you'd get to spend on your priorities if you cut back your phone/computer/online time.

WRITE HERE

Redefine what "balance" means to you. Write out your definition. Include concrete examples of exactly what it looks and feels like to you.

3. YOU CAN STILL BE HAPPY. Sometimes, things don't work out or go as planned. Keep the faith and find a way to be happy anyway. Don't let the disappointments and the unmet expectations mean more than they do.

Yes, it sucks when you do everything "right" and it still all crumbles to the ground.

You plan, get your mind right, and take action…and nope. For whatever reason, it all falls apart. Whhhhhhhy?

That's just how life rolls.

You don't always lose the weight, find true love, have the baby, travel the world or get the promotion. It sucks. It may even be completely heartbreaking. But it doesn't have to be the end of your story.

You can still find a way to be happy.
To enjoy your life. To do great things.

It might not look how you thought it would, but that doesn't mean it's game over.

Take the time to grieve. To feel it all. And to let your heart break wide open. *Do not, under any circumstances, skip this step.*

Then, when you're ready, or maybe even a little before, decide to put your pieces back together in a new and different way. Find a new version of happiness. A new focus. A new purpose.

You may never be the same, but you don't have to be. You're not actually supposed to be. But you can still find a way forward. You can find a way to smile and to laugh again. You can rewrite your happily ever after.

Grieve what's gone and find your way forward. Be happy anyway. And do it because this is *your one life*. You deserve it. You're meant to be here and to feel fully alive while you are. Make the most of this one very precious chance you've got. Don't waste anymore time.

DO THIS

Sometimes, we feel guilty. Or like it's not fair, okay or right to be happy. The thing is, life is really short and it's filled with contradictions. While it's up to you to decide what you want your experience of it to be like, you may feel like you need permission from someone to do so.

So ask yourself, "Who do I, or might I, need permission from and what do I (or what could I possibly) need permission for?"

Then, imagine asking for that permission. What are the conditions that would allow you to get it?

Examples:

- Someone you love who is struggling: It feels selfish to be happy knowing she is hurting. I need to trust that my happiness isn't hurting her, maybe it even brings her some joy.

- Someone you love has died: It doesn't feel right being happy without that person. I need to believe that it's okay to be happy and sad at the same time. And that he has always wanted happiness for me, now is no different.
- Someone you love who is sick: It doesn't seem fair to be happy while this person is dealing with something so scary. I need to see that my happiness fuels my energy, which actually allows me to support this person in a more powerful way.

What do you think this person would want for you? Is it actually fair that you're stopping your happiness on his or her behalf? Is this what he or she would actually even want?

WRITE HERE

What would it mean to you to "be happy anyway"? How do you feel about this idea?

4. YOU DESERVE TO LIVE A HAPPY LIFE. Just because you do. You deserve it, and you're worthy of it, and that's exactly why you're here. It's why you were given the gift of life. It truly is that simple. And it's the truth for every single one of us.

Think of Earth as your giant playground. Sure, there might be some shitty kids around, things that you're not sure about or that freak you out a little. You might even trip and fall flat on your face. But you get up, dust the mulch off and get back at it. No big deal!

Because you know you belong. You're meant to be here. And you're meant to explore, experience, learn, laugh and play.

You're meant to fall down sometimes.
And you're meant to keep getting back up.

You are here, surrounded by amazing things. Simple everyday life things so that you can play, laugh and have fun. Give yourself the chance to see, and truly enjoy, what's right there in front of you.

Live your life. Play on the freaking playground.

DO THIS

Make a list of all the things that made you smile or laugh out loud as a kid. All the things you did to play.

••• *Ideas: riding your bike with no hands, catching lightning bugs, playing dress-up, swinging on a swing, making s'mores, playing outside, skipping stones, swimming with your friends, howling at the full moon, baking chocolate chip cookies, etc.* •••

Remember the simple, easily accessible things that you once did, _and probably still do_, that make you happy.

Then, go through your list and circle the ones you could do now. It's okay if you have a more "adult" version of the activity (yard games exist for a reason). The purpose is to do the things that make you smile, laugh and feel happy. That let you be playful. So

---

that you can tap back into that part of you and see just how easily accessible those things are to you!

As a kid, I loved to...

_____

_____

_____

_____

_____

WRITE HERE

If it's true that you actually deserve to live a happy life, one that feels light and free, and is full of laughter, fun and play, what would change?

5. DON'T GET SO FOCUSED ON WHAT YOU WANT THAT YOU FORGET WHAT YOU'VE GOT. We've all been there, done that. Focused in on this new, exciting thing you want. You can see it so clearly...it's right there. But still out of reach.

You're in that in-between space where you're soooooooooo close, but not quite there yet. You're doing all the things to get you to where you want to go. You're making progress and moving forward. But when you take a look around, it's not yours yet.

Then, you start to compare what you have to what you want. And what you have starts to feel like it's just not good enough anymore. You wish for things to be different.

Stop. Take a step back. Remember that *what you have right now happens to also be something you once wanted.* Something you hoped for and dreamed about. Something you worked towards. Something that felt new and exciting.

It's okay to want more. But your more is best served as a bonus to the great things you've already got going on. When you forget how good things are, or can be, as-is, you risk getting caught up in the constant chase for the next thing. And you'll forever be chasing because there will *always* be a next thing.

But when you're happy with what you have first. When you appreciate it and see the value in it. When you remember what it took you to get to here, then you go for more and know that no matter what happens, you're already so, so good.

DO THIS

Look around at what you have right now that was once a hope, want, wish or dream.

Write it here:

Remember what it was like to want it. What felt exciting about it? What sparked the desire?

Write some notes here:

_____

_____

_____

_____

Remember and reconnect with that now.

<u>**WRITE HERE**</u>

What do you need so you can know that who you are and what you have are already more than enough _while also_ going for more? How can you find peace with where you are AND hope for where you're going?

 6. YOU GET TO BE HAPPY, TOO. You get to love and to laugh and to do all the things that make your heart happy. You get to enjoy your life. To make your dreams come true. And to have _all_ that is good.

You get to feel good, do amazing things and be happy. You get to fill in the blank with whatever it is you want because you get to be, do and have all of those things (and more), too.

And you get to *simply because you do*. That's it. No prerequisites. No hidden conditions. No drama. You exist; therefore, you get to.

So, stop questioning if happiness is meant for you. Stop feeling guilty about wanting more. And stop blaming and beating yourself up for things in the past, things that are gone and things that were never up to you to control.

You get to have it all. You get to be so freaking happy simply because you do.

Decide—that you get to be happy, too. Decide that while things might not ever be perfect, your life can still be amazing. (It's probably way more amazing right now than you even realize.)

And decide that miracles are meant for you, too.

Once you do that, take a deep breath. And finally let all that goodness in. Let yourself feel what it's like to be happy. To believe that it's possible. And to trust that yes, it's for you, too.

DO THIS

Now that you've decided that you get to be happy, too, look around. What opportunities for bringing in happiness do you see?

•••*Ideas: Perfect yard for a dog (something you've always wanted)? Go find your fur baby! Great natural lighting? Open the blinds/curtains/ windows and instantly brighten up that room. A beautiful vintage tea set? Invite your neighbor over for some tea and to chat.•••*

Look around you to see where you can let more of the goodness in.

Pick one thing. Do it today!

Opportunities to let the goodness/happiness/light in:

_____

_____

_____

_____

WRITE HERE

In what ways have you been keeping out the things that make you smile or feel happy? Are you ready to let them in? Why or why not?

7. BE GRATEFUL FOR WHAT YOU HAVE; STOP CHASING WHAT YOU DON'T. Chasing is exhausting. Even if it gets you to where you think you want to go, there's really no end to it. There's always going to be something you don't have. Something new and something next. There's always going to be so much to go for or to go after.

When you're always caught up in the chase, you miss out on so much. You miss out on all that you've got going for you. On all the goodness that's already right there at your fingertips. And you miss out because you're hiding, avoiding or trying to fix something that can't actually be fixed by the thing you're chasing.

And then one day, you'll look back on all that chasing and realize that you missed out on appreciating, enjoying and celebrating what you had when you had it. That you forgot to really show up and live in your "good old days."

So, stay grounded in what you've got. In all the amazing people, places and things you've already surrounded yourself with. *Let yourself live in these moments.* Sit in the stillness. Know that these things are yours. And you are theirs.

You belong to each other. You're part of the same. Trust in that. Don't run from it. Trust that you deserve it. And that you get to have it all. Start by letting yourself enjoy the life you're already living. Slow down. Settle in. Breathe.

You're here because you're meant to be here. This is all yours because it is. You get what's next because you do. Show up. Do your part. Let it all in.

Chasing is not required—*valuing, appreciating and living are.*

See it all again like it's the first time. Like it's all new. See the value, the beauty, and the amazingness that already fills up your life. Remember why it all matters. And how you got here.

See all that's working.

Your heart is beating, your lungs are breathing, and your eyes are seeing. These things matter. They're a big freaking deal! If you're not sure where to start, start here.

Be grateful. Be happy. Start with the simplest things. See the amazingness that exists in the mundane, simple, every day. Stop taking all the people, places, experiences and things that are so readily accessible to you for granted. Make eye contact. Listen. Pay attention.

All that you're chasing isn't going to fix things or fill you up. You've got to do that first. You've got to be good first. And once you do it, then you'll be able to see all that's right there. You'll be able to sit in the stillness. To show up. To pay attention, to feel and to appreciate.

Be thankful for all the little things, and for all those big things you've forgotten about. Be thankful for all that's already right there. *And let them matter more* than all that you don't have.

Then, and only then, go for more.

When you're seeing, celebrating and excited about what you already have, you go for more without needing the more. You feel calm, confident and at ease. You're not chasing or desperate because you're already good. Soooo good! Everything else is like a beautiful bonus to this pretty great life you're already living.

DO THIS

When you first wake up, think of one thing you're grateful for. *Maybe it's a good night of sleep, comfortable bed, safe home, waking up for another day, the person (or pet) next to you, your lungs for breathing, something you're looking forward to, the sunshine— whatever comes to mind.*

When you start your day like this, you'll notice more and more things that are working in your life. Every time you notice something, say thank you, thank you, thank you!

Practice seeing, celebrating, living, feeling, letting in and remembering all the good things you already have. These are your "good old days." Live them before they're gone.

Today, I am grateful for...

_____

_____

_____

_____

WRITE HERE

What's the chasing actually doing for you? In what ways might it be protecting you (keeping you safe, distracted or playing small)?

Your first response might be "It's not!" Okay, but if it were...just consider the possibility for a moment and free-write whatever comes to you.

....

8. CELEBRATE EVERYONE AND EVERYTHING AS OFTEN AS POSSIBLE. Celebrating is one of the greatest gifts in life. Celebrate others and let others celebrate you.

We're all in this life together. It's not you versus me. It's we—_you AND me_. Always. We're on the same team, even if we don't agree on all things.

If someone else has what you want, they're not taking it from you. There's more than enough to go around. They're just proving to you what's possible. They are _your evidence_ for what you can have.

So, cheer for each other. Root for everyone to win, to go big and to take the risks. Encourage people to go all in on life. To go for their dreams. And to do great things. Be there, support it, celebrate it.

Don't judge. Don't make it about you. _Be willing to show up for them, too._

We can't all win all the things all the time. But we can show up, do our best and appreciate one another. And we can get inspired by people who are willing to do the same.

Someone going for her dreams and doing big things means you can, too. Sure, there are assholes everywhere. BUT most people are really good. _Choose to see the good in the ones who have it._ Look for them. Surround yourself with them. Be one of them!!!

And then, cheer them on. Let them cheer you on. Celebrate your wins, and all the things you possibly can, along the way. It'll make the journey more fun and much more meaningful.

DO THIS

Today, give someone a high five for going big, for taking a risk, for falling down AND getting back up, for showing up strong or for doing something great.

Look for every opportunity to cheer on a colleague, friend, family member, or fellow human. High fives, clapping and woooohooos are always a good idea.

Bonus points for high-fiving someone you often feel like you're competing against. This can mean someone at work or on the pickleball court. Competition can bring out the best in us when we let it!

Who'd you high five?   **How'd they inspire you?**

WRITE HERE

How do you feel when you see someone taking risks, succeeding, or getting what she wants? Tell the truth…

9. HOW YOU FEEL MATTERS. If your body aches, it's hard to *do* things—to feel motivated, to have energy and to take action. If your brain feels foggy, it's hard to *create*—to really see things, to problem solve and to consider. If you're constantly distracted, it's hard to *believe*—to trust and to keep the faith.

The bottom line is if you don't feel good, it's hard to be *happy*— to be present, to enjoy things and to engage in life.

So do what makes you feel good. Pay attention to your body, mind and spirit. Take care of all parts of your being.

Know what makes you feel good, and <u>do those things</u>.

Not the quick, cheap and easy, short-lived kinda feel good, but the really deep down, all parts of you, "let's make it last" kinda feel good. The things that energize your soul, nourish your body, and inspire your mind.

Know what these things are for you. Prioritize them. Because when you feel good, it's a whole lot easier to be happy. To show up, to say yes and to do the things you actually want to do.

So eat the bright, vibrant, colorful and yes, delicious foods. Turn up the music and dance your ass off. Wear the clothes that feel good. Read the books that make you go hmmmm. Do ALL of the things that turn you on. That light you up. And that truly, genuinely feel good to you.

Because how you feel matters. It makes all the difference in the kind of life you're able to live. Surround yourself, as much as possible, with the people, experiences and things that make you feel good. Set yourself up to succeed, to feel amazing, to have it all and to truly be happy.

Do it for you and for every single other person in your life. _Because how you feel is what you radiate out into this world._ And the world needs a strong, vibrant you!

DO THIS

Create a list of all the things that feel good to you, that truly nourish you. Break down your list into categories:

- Mind (_examples: reading the New York Times or taking a class to learn how to speak Italian, to cook, or something interesting and new to you_)
- Body (_examples: mango smoothies, eating fresh berries, daily dance parties, playing golf, morning stretches or walks outside_)
- Spirit (_examples: meditating, volunteer work or going to church_)
- Life (_examples: vacation, visiting family or friends, date nights, working on passion projects_)

These categories might overlap or flow into each other—that's totally fine. This is just a helpful way to organize your ideas.

Commit to doing one thing from each category today.

Think about how you can build your routines around these things.

Love to journal and drink coffee? Start your mornings off that way! It's so much easier to get up earlier to do things you love and genuinely enjoy.

Do the things that make you feel good. That nourish you, set you up for success and let you thrive!

My feel good list:

Mind

Body

Spirit

Life

WRITE HERE

When you look at your list of things that feel good, how do they actually feel to you? Do they feel important? Do they feel easy or hard? Are they actually things you want to do? Do you feel excited? Overwhelmed? Curious? Frivolous? Are you surprised that life actually gets to be/feel good?

10. A POSITIVE MINDSET IS ONLY AS POWERFUL AS YOUR BELIEF IN IT. You can't trick your thoughts to be different from your beliefs *no matter how hard you try.*

Your thoughts come from your beliefs—like branches that come from the trunk of a tree. You will always circle back to what you fundamentally believe to be true.

If there are thoughts you want to change—thoughts that are negative, limiting, painful or bothersome in some way—you're going to have to learn to change the beliefs that are behind those thoughts.

The good news is that you get to decide what you believe to be true. The bad news is that a lot of times, your true beliefs (especially the most painful ones) are hidden deep below the surface.

You've become so good at trying to fake your way through life that you're not even sure what those beliefs are. Besides, they're raw and painful—you don't actually want to face them—so you do your best not to.

But there's a part of you that wants to change. A part of you that wants to know what it needs to know so it can do what it needs to do. There's also a part of you that wants to keep things exactly the same. A part that's scared some horrible thing you believe about yourself may actually be true.

You worry that if you bring that deep hidden belief up to the surface and really look at it, what scares you the most about yourself will become your new reality. So you avoid it, stuff it down, and tune it out.

Here's the thing you don't know: just because you have a thought or belief, doesn't make it true. The belief you're worried about was most likely put in your brain when you were young, vulnerable or scared. And it's probably not even accurate or valid. It was skewed by emotion, perception and age—along with a lot of other factors.

> You need to know that it's safe now to pull that belief out and examine it. You can handle it. And your thoughts can guide you there.

Use your thoughts as a window to look in to see what you believe to be true about yourself and the world. Let them guide you so that you can pull out, look at and finally see what the beliefs are that are leading you astray. And so that you can change whatever it is you need and want to change.

Faking it won't work forever. Odds are it's not working that great now. And until you find the courage to look at and to change those deep, hidden beliefs, there will always be a piece of you that's missing and hiding out.

Take a deep breath and do what you need to do. It's time to set yourself free from all that worry, fear and self doubt *(that's not even real, right or true)* so you can be who you are and live as you're meant to live.

DO THIS

Start a thought tracker. Write down the thoughts you'd like to change. Especially as they relate to being who you are and having what you want in life. Start to notice categories or themes that come up. Get curious and ask yourself some follow up questions.

Example:

Want: I want to start a business.

Tho´ughts: I don't know how to start a business. It's too hard. I can't do that. Who's going to buy from me? I don't even know what I'm doing. I never have any good ideas. I'm so dumb sometimes. Ugh, why can't I ever figure anything out?!

Questions: What lets me know this is hard? When did I decide that I can't do hard things? Where/from whom did I first receive that message? What evidence do I have that it's true (examples from your life—experiences/what people said to you)? What are the beliefs I have about this? Are they true?

Belief: I'm not good enough. I'm dumb. Things are hard for me.

Is it true? No! Sometimes things are hard but all things aren't hard for me! There are plenty of things that come really easily to me—like cooking—I'm a great cook!

As you go, examples of events that support or validate the same belief may start to come to you. *For example, my kindergarten teacher had me stand up in front of the class "as an example" when I didn't know the alphabet. I felt stupid and humiliated. I knew right then and there that things everyone else could do would always be hard for me (supporting the belief "things are hard for me").*

The more examples you have that point you to the same belief, the more likely you're dealing with one of your primary beliefs—which is exactly what you want to be working with!

The goal here is to uncover the belief and ask yourself, "Is it true?" Odds are pretty good that you can look at that belief now and poke some holes in it. That's all you need to do to loosen the vice grip you unknowingly have on that belief, which creates the space for new, more-true-to-you beliefs to come in!

Thought Tracker

Want:

Thoughts:

Questions:

Beliefs:

Is it true?

WRITE HERE

If self-doubt, worry and fear were completely gone, who would you now be and what would you do?

11. IMPERFECT, MESSY AND DON'T GIVE A F*CK! You are worthy of what you want—exactly as you are. It doesn't matter how messy and imperfect you think you are, you still get to be, do and have great things in your life.

So, forgive yourself!!! There's no use in holding on to all that baggage. Let yourself off the hook. And let all that's happened up to this point just be what it is.

Accept who you are as you are. Accept your life exactly as it is in this moment. Find some peace. Know that everything is okay. Know that *you are okay.*

Even though you have regrets. Even though things didn't go as planned. And even though sometimes, you're afraid, full of doubt and totally unsure.

You fucking got this. *You can still live your life on your terms starting right now.* You can still do great things. It's not too late—there is still time!!!

Just decide that you are no longer willing to let the bits and pieces of your past, and of who you once were, define you or this moment anymore.

Set yourself free. Let it all be okay.

Then, step into the imperfection and the mess. But don't worry so much about it. Dare to dream a new dream from right here, right now. Find your peace and let it fuel you forward.

Trust that you are worthy and deserving BECAUSE you exist. BECAUSE you are here. That's it. That's all it takes. You are here now, so show up right here, right now.

You have the opportunity that not everyone gets. Don't squander it by dwelling and doubting.

Instead, be grateful. Take advantage. Don't get caught up in the drama.

You get to decide if, when, what or how your stuff defines you. *You* decide if it gives you a perspective that holds you back or perspective that pulls you forward. *You* decide if it breaks you down or makes you better. *You* decide if it shuts you off or sets you free. And *you* decide whether or not it let's you light this big beautiful world of ours on fire.

DO THIS

Create a mindset mantra. It's a short statement to help you remember that mess and imperfection don't actually disqualify you from living a great life. You can find your peace and let what you want define you.

Some examples:
- It's absolutely possible to live a messy, imperfect life and still be happy.
- It's completely safe for me to make peace with the past. It's time to let go.
- I am worthy/deserving/good enough simply because I exist.
- I decide who I am and what defines me.
- Yes, there is still plenty of time.

Use these mindset mantras to help you shift your perspective and to remember that you define you.

My mindset mantras:

WRITE HERE

In what ways has wanting or needing to *"do things 'right' or not at all"* stopped you from doing anything? What if you let it be okay to do things imperfectly and to be okay with being imperfect, how might you do things differently? What might you try?

----

 12. COMPARISON HIJACKS HAPPINESS. Every. Single. Time. You don't actually need to look outside of yourself for anything—ever. Sure, it can help to see "how" others are doing things in order to get the ideas flowing. Or to gather information and learn from the experts. But you still have to trust yourself enough to send all that information through *your own filter*.

You are your own best expert on you. On what matters to you most. On what you want. And on how you're living.

Confidence, happiness, connection and a sense of purpose—all of that comes from within. You validate you. You trust in you. And the quicker you realize that, the better off you'll be!

DO THIS

Take a break from outsourcing. Focus on what *you know*, and trust in that information. Today, do this by NOT referring to any of your electronic devices for _any_ information. No recipe look-up, no "in what year did x, y and z happen?" and no searching for any how-to tutorials.

If you need to, make a list of your questions and set aside a designated amount of time tomorrow (15-20 minutes) to research. Set the timer so you don't end up going down the virtual rabbit hole and end up spending hours online.

Notes on how it went:

_____

_____

_____

_____

_____

WRITE HERE

In what areas of your life do you look for "advice"? Are you truly consulting, learning and gathering information OR are you actually looking for validation?

13. ANYTHING'S POSSIBLE, MIRACLES HAPPEN EVERY DAY. If you don't believe this, *it's because you're not seeing them.* You've got to choose to see them first. They're happening all around you all the time. The miracles your body performs. The miracles in nature. The miracles from human kindness.

You are surrounded by beautiful, amazing, great and miraculous things—always.

But you have to be willing to see them first. You have to know that they're possible. *You can't see what you don't believe.*

Your experiences will confirm your thoughts. *What you believe to be true will fill your life.* So, set your beliefs accordingly! Choose exactly what you want to see. And start to look around as all those miracles unfold.

DO THIS

Put both hands on your heart. Say out loud, "I believe that anything's possible and miracles happen every day."

Notice how this feels in your body. If true and good, then write down at least one miracle you witnessed today.

If this doesn't feel true and good for you, revisit the exercise in #10!

Miracle(s) I witnessed today:

_____

_____

_____

_____

WRITE HERE

Do you believe that anything's possible for you? How about for other people? Do the beliefs you have for yourself match the ones you have for others?

....

14. IF YOU WANT TO BE HAPPY, GO BE HAPPY. Focus on what you want. Focus on what feels good. Focus on your strengths, what you're good at and your wins. This is how you can go and be happy.

You set the intention and you do the things that actually make you feel that way. *And you stop doing the things that don't.*

You stop focusing on your weaknesses, your struggles and your areas "in need of improvement." And you stop doing the things you hate doing.

You set boundaries. You focus on what works. *And you do the things you actually can do. That you want to do. That feel good, that light you up and that make you happy.*

See the function and the purpose in all things. Choose to not get caught up in the drama. Set your priorities and act accordingly.

It really is that simple.

*Know what makes you happy
so you can do what makes you happy.*

DO THIS

Pick one thing on your regular to do list that hijacks your happiness (you hate it or it drains your energy).

Stop doing it!

Let it be that easy.

Task(s) that hijacks my happy or drains my energy:

_____

_____

_____

WRITE HERE

What keeps you doing things you don't want to do? And what stops you from doing things you actually do want to do? What steps can you take to turn that around?

Recap

Success is getting what you want.
Happiness is wanting what you get.
—Dale Carnegie

You've got to do the work before you can make the choice to be happy anyway. It's just the way it goes. But the work is an amazing opportunity.

It's a chance to get to know yourself again. To reconnect with who you truly are. *To focus on what matters to you most.* To wholeheartedly trust in yourself. To let go of what's gone. To dream a new dream. And to see that *you absolutely can* do the things you want to do.

You have the capacity to do all of this, but <u>you have to know it</u> in order to be able to make the choice to be happy anyway.

Being happy anyway is a decision. It's a mindset. It's a way of life. It's a willingness to step into the unknown. To let things be what they are. To not only count on yourself, but to anchor in to what you believe in. To know that you don't need things to be all sunshiny and perfect in order to be happy.

You get to be happy by living your life in your own way. And by creating a life that is a beautiful and honest expression of you. There are no rules. There are no expectations. Just you showing up in your life, every single day, exactly as you are.

You've done the work, now go make the choice. Be happy anyway.

Remember...

Take 5-10 minutes now to write your responses below.

My big takeaways:

_____

_____

_____

Something that surprised me:

_____

_____

_____

To help me to choose to be happy anyway, I:

_____

_____

_____

What I _can_ (and want to) do now:

_____

_____

_____

The 1-2 "Do This" activities I'll continue:

1. _____

2. _____

That's a wrap!

CONGRATULATIONS!!! You should be feeling pretty badass right now. You've done something most people don't do— *you showed up for yourself.* You decided that you matter. That your happiness matters. And you did something about it.

You decided to reconnect with *who you truly are,* with who you've always been. And to dream a new dream from this place. To stop listening to all the naysayers, old stories and shitty beliefs that were keeping you stuck. To *shake things up and turn things around* so that you could get into action and make some magic happen in your life.

You've created a ripple effect. You've changed this world just by becoming more you.

That's pretty freaking cool! I am beyond grateful that there are people like you in this world. And I am really proud that this book that you're holding in your hands connects us. Thank you for letting me into your world and for letting this book be part of your journey.

They say all good things must come to an end, and while that may be true, those endings always lead us to new beginnings. I hope that this book has helped you find your new beginning—one that feels real and exciting and most importantly, completely true to you.

Because in the end, that's all that really matters. *This is your one life.* You're the only one who has to feel good about how you're living it. So, be who you are and let the truth in that radiate out into this world. Let it be a messy, imperfect and beautiful expression of exactly who you are!

Until next time!

Emily xox

P.S. If you're ready for "next time" right now, read on....

What's next?

Next steps are much easier than first steps, which is why it's so, so important to keep that momentum going! You've taken 10 weeks' worth of steps. You've finished this book, and now you're ready for your next step. It's time to take all the new insights you've gained during this really important self-discovery process and put them to good use.

Maybe you know exactly what's next for you, but you're not quite sure what to do about it. Maybe you have a much stronger sense of who you want to be and what you want to create, but you're not quite clear about exactly what to do next. Or maybe you're at a fork in the road, not quite sure which way to go.

When I started my business, Balance & Thrive, back in 2012, I knew that I wanted to do things differently. I knew that I wanted a different experience for my clients and myself, but I didn't know exactly what that meant. I just knew I had to take the first step, so I took it. With each step I took, the next one became clearer to me. So, I just kept doing that—taking one step at a time.

And over the years, my business and my life have continued to evolve. With each new phase (basically every year), I've taken a step back to recalibrate. I've checked in to see where I've been, who I've become, what I want to create and where I want to go next.

As humans, we are fluid beings—*always changing and growing*. And this life we live is a dynamic experience filled with so many unexpected things. Because of this, we need to get good at adapting, at trusting in who we are and what we want, and at doing our part.

When you're good at these things, you're able to get who you are, what you want and how you live in sync at any point in time. That is happiness. Your ability to create it is invaluable because it defines how you experience this one life you get to live.

You've had the chance now to dive into some self-discovery. You've connected with the core of who you are, played around with your dreams and desires, and considered the reality that there is still time for you to do the things you want to do *as of this moment.* You've decided *to decide,* to become undone and to truly step into who you are—messy, imperfect and exactly right.

You've learned how to _embrace the contradictions_ that exist in your life, to let go of what's gone, and to go around (or through) the things that are stopping you or getting in your way. You've become clearer on what matters to you most, on what you're saying yes to, and you've become more confident in *your ability to impact your own life.*

And you now know that *you, too, can be happy anyway.*

The steps you've taken, regardless of which ones or in what order, are important. All that you've done up to this point matters—because you matter. *How you live creates a ripple effect into this world.* You can see now how small hinges (little actions you can do in a day) swing big doors (impact your day to day life and how you feel).

And now you're ready for your next step, which is where the *Laugh More, Live Louder* course comes in. This is a year-long group mentorship program to help you get crystal clear on what's next for you, and to confidently take the steps to make it happen.

This course is for you if you're ready to cut the bullshit, strip away all the nonsense and really get down to it. What is it that you actually _do_ want, and how are you going to get there?

If you're someone who is willing to look inside yourself and the world around you so that you can make some changes and really truly create a life that feels happy and fulfilling, this experience is for you.

At this point, you know me and my style quite well. I'm a no-nonsense, let's-not-sugarcoat-things kinda gal. I will have your back, I will hold your hand and I will cheer you on. But I can't do any of these things if you're not willing to show up strong for yourself.

(By reading this book, you are already saying that you are that kind of person. You are willing to show up for yourself, and you're ready to stop going through the motions and really truly say YES to creating the kind of life you want to live. You're smart, savvy and motivated. But maybe, you're just not quite sure about what it is you want, let alone how to get there!)

During this year-long course, you'll learn specific step-by-step strategies so you can clearly see what you want, get rid of what doesn't work, and have a little fun along the way as you create the kind of life you actually want to live. That means accepting some things and changing others. It means letting go of what's gone and stepping into what's here for you right now.

The *Laugh More, Live Louder* course will help you do exactly that.

While I am absolutely a fan of positive psychology and I genuinely believe that gratitude is a fundamental piece to living a happy life, I don't believe that the buck stops there. Real life is messy and complicated. Relationships, expectations, loss—they are all real and you can't fix or put a positive spin on those things. The good news is that you don't actually have to!

You can be sad and happy at the same time. They don't cancel one another out. You can grieve your losses and smile at the good times. Embracing this "mess" is one of the key teachings in the course.

You get to experience the full range of all the things in your life. Start by giving yourself permission to do so! When you do, you actually free yourself up to be in the present. To do what you want. And to bring your dreams to life.

The *Laugh More, Live Louder* course teaches you the <u>exact strategies</u> to do this. It provides you with clearly outlined, concrete directions along with handouts so you can practice using your own, personal examples. And it incorporates a group coaching component so you can ask questions, get the support and accountability you need to stay on track, and break through your blocks.

Achieving your goals takes work. You've got to be willing to show up and say yes time and time again (even when it means saying no to other important things). It can feel hard sometimes, but it's nothing you can't handle—especially when you have a system in place that goes along with you every step of the way!

THE COURSE

* * * *Read below for more details about the course. If you're ready to sign up, head over to balancethrive.com/laughmorelivelouder.* * * *

The *Laugh More, Live Louder* year-long course expands on the work we've done together in this book. We'll go through the seasons together so that you fully understand how to match your action to your energy (one of the fundamental principles in this course). You're going to get a completely new understanding of how to achieve your goals and you'll feel a lot better about what you've got going on in your life.

Using the different tools and strategies in the course, you will learn how to change the layers of all the things you want to change. The course is all about implementation, and you will learn how to create a system that's uniquely fitted to you and your life. This is _not_ about simply using someone else's system—it's about creating your own. That way, it'll actually work for you! And you'll learn ways of doing things that you will refer back to forever!

WHY THE SEASONS?

Do you ever wonder why it's so hard to get yourself motivated in the winter? Or why cleaning and organizing in the spring feels like the exact right thing to do? Or why your energy is so high in the summer?

Well, there's a season for everything. And one of the fundamental mistakes that most of us make is not leveraging the energy of the seasons with the actions we're taking in our day-to-day life.

We're so used to forcing ourselves and pushing through that we end up feeling drained and depleted really, really fast. That's why your great New Year's resolutions have you feeling deflated and disappointed with yourself (and life) before the first week of February.

When you learn how to match your action to the season you're in, you become massively more productive AND quite honestly, so much happier.

The **winter season** is the time to settle in and cozy up. It's the season of turning inward, of resting, restoring, and reconnecting.

And it's the perfect time to reflect on the year that's passed and what's up ahead.

When you take the time to look back, to learn, to reconnect and to *be thoughtful about where you've been and where you're headed,* you create a strong foundation from which to build. This is a key element in creating happiness and success.

The **spring season** is the time to "prepare the soil and plant the seed." It's the season of shedding, of letting go, of renewal, of anticipation and of stepping into. And it's the perfect time to clear out the clutter and create a new framework.

When you take the time to do this, you make it easier to take action that *feels right (and you decrease the chances of sabotaging yourself down the road).* You get your mind, body, spirit *and your life* on the same page. You resolve any lingering conflicts and you step into what's next. You make it easier for yourself to move forward—to grow—with a sense of ease, confidence and freedom.

The **summer season** is the time when energy is high. The days are longer, and it's easier to get up and get going. It's the season of movement. And it's the perfect time to get focused and into action.

Your energy is at its highest in this season, which means you'll have a better capacity to learn new things and to do things differently. When you take the time to start new habits and build in new routines now, you're more likely to succeed, and they'll be easier for you to continue throughout the year.

The **fall season** is the time when you start to take a step back and to really let everything settle. It's the season of slowing down and recalibrating. And it's the perfect time to check in with yourself, to see if who you are being is a match for what you want, and to make any adjustments you need to.

This is the season of self-care, of refocusing your attention to what matters to you the most and of appreciating what you have. It's the time when you feel like all of your pieces really come together and you get to truly see, enjoy and appreciate all that you've created and how far you've come.

Understanding your energy
and matching your action to it is by far one of
the most profound shifts you will make in your life.

And the cool thing is, you can start this process at any point in time. You don't have to wait until January 1st to get going. You can start in whatever season you're in right now!!!

Each of the seasons overlap and flow into one another. You just have to trust in the timing and believe that you are starting at the exact right place for you. This is also a fundamental teaching in the course. You don't have to do all the things all the time or in a certain order, but you do have to **trust that you get what you need when you need it.** And remember: you can always circle back.

THE MEMBERSHIP SITE

The *Laugh More, Live Louder* membership site is preloaded with an extensive library of resources. Upon joining, you have instant 24/7 access to the site where you'll find exclusive audio and video trainings, supplemental handouts and exercises, tons of guided visualizations and meditations, weekly journal prompts, and so much more!

Like all things, this course continues to grow and evolve. For the most up-to-date information about course logistics, ways to access support, specific content information, bonus modules, live group coaching and more, please refer to the website.

Get all the details and join the course at:

balancethrive.com/laughmorelivelouder

Hope to see you there!

Emily

If you're not quite ready for the course, no problem. A great next step for you would be to reach out and get connected either on Facebook @BalanceAndThrive or on Instagram @balancethrive.

Be sure to hop on the newsletter list so you can stay up-to-date with the latest information, special offers and coaching tips, tricks and inspiration over at **balancethrive.com/lifeyouwant**

And don't forget to go get all the *Happiness Happens* exclusive bonus downloads at **balancethrive.com/hhdownloads.**

Book Club It

Brunch, cocktails, books and conversation—some of my favorite things wrapped up into one amazing event: a Happiness Happens Book Club!

My closest girlfriends are the ones I don't see or talk to often, but when we do, within 10 minutes, we're diving into the deep stuff in a fun and lighthearted way. There are never any judgments, no attempts to "fix" anything, no "I know more than you," and no unsolicited advice. Just real, down-to-earth, meaningful conversations.

And this book is the perfect complement to that kind of dynamic!

Not only do you get to dive into some really important conversations, but you also get to explore this information from different viewpoints and real-life examples. You get to *put into practice what you're working on* in a safe way with a group you trust. You get to have people, who know what you're up to and are doing the same thing, in your corner, cheering you on and calling you out.

Support, accountability and inspiration will make your Happiness Happens journey that much more powerful!

So, gather up a few friends *who you know* will show up for this experience in the same way that you will, and get together once a month for 3 months. This gives you a container of time to work through the book within a clear framework, while also giving you just a pinch of flexibility.

Yes, you want to think, reflect, explore, discuss and consider, but not too much that you forget to take action. *Action is key.* Stick to the time frame and keep moving! Make sure your group is up for getting focused and taking action. And you're all willing to call each other out with some tough love and accountability!

SUGGESTED BOOK CLUB FRAMEWORK (3-PART SERIES)

1. Read through the Introduction and skim the Table of Contents prior to your **first meeting.** At the first meeting, talk about what prompted you to read the book and create/join the book club. Set an intention for the experience.

   This is also a great time to lay some ground rules and get on the same page with your expectations. It's always a good idea to get the logistics out of the way right off the bat.

   Questions:
   - What prompted you to read *Happiness Happens*?
   - What are you most excited about with this book?
   - What intention/focus/goal do you have for this experience?
   - Which step or section seems most exciting to you?
   - What guidelines, ground rules and expectations would help you get the most out of this experience?

2. During the **second meeting**, you'll be about midway through the book. Discuss the topics you've read, actions you've taken and new insights you've gained.

   Questions:
   - What's been your biggest new insight?
   - Which action did you most enjoy?

- Which action has helped you the most? In what way?
- What's your focus for the rest of the book?

3. During the **third and final meeting**, you'll be done with the book. Discuss your 2-week reviews from the end of each of the sections.

Questions:
- Which actions did you decide to continue?
- What's been your biggest new insight or aha?
- What's changed?

••• Download the full book club reader guide at
balancethrive.com/hhdownloads •••

If you would like me to be a guest at your event, head over to balancethrive.com/contact and fill out the contact form. This is also where you can send booking inquiries.

Q&A with Emily

Are you happy?

Ha! Great question. Yes, overall, I'm really happy. But how I define happiness may not be the same as how you define it. For me, happiness isn't a permanent state. I have days and moments that are hard, but I have more happy moments than not.

Things definitely aren't perfect, but they're mostly good…and I'm good with that.

What does happiness mean to you?

I am not a sunshiny, rainbows and unicorn kind of person. Quite honestly, the hard push with all the positive psychology and the gratitude all day every day stuff drives me crazy. It doesn't feel real, attainable or sustainable to me—even though I strongly believe in a lot of the elements of it. I just don't work that way. It's not my operating system and I don't want it or need it to be.

And because I don't work that way, I felt for a long time that I wasn't or couldn't be happy. That all my stuff meant happiness wasn't available to me. But that's not at all true.

Yes, I practice gratitude and yes, I integrate a lot of elements from positive psychology. I believe strongly in focusing on your strengths and your potential solutions. But I also know all of that coexists with all sorts of other things.

It's messy, I'm imperfect and life can feel hard some days, but I'm okay with that. It doesn't mean anything. It's life. And like my Papa always used to say, "This, too, shall pass."

For me, that's all part of how I define happiness. It's about embracing the whole range of stuff. Letting the hard things be hard and the good things be good. To wake up each day and do my best to do what makes me happy, to be around the people I love and to smile. And to try not to get caught up in the drama (that's kind of my kryptonite).

My son is also a huge source of happiness for me. I love being his mom and he makes it easy for me to smile often throughout the day.

What's your #1 happiness tip?

Figure out who you are and be that person as much as possible.

What do you think gets in the way of people being happy?

Short answer: fear, control, lies and self-doubt.

We get in the habit of believing things that aren't true—that we're not good enough, that we can't have the things we want in life, that we don't deserve to be happy, that being happy is selfish or unimportant, that it requires perfection or keeping it all together.

And these stories usually come from a well-meaning place. But they're just not true.

Your happiness matters. It's okay to want and to have it. It's not selfish or frivolous. It's not taking away from anyone else. And it's totally accessible to every single one of us.

It's actually the thing that will make you a better human. It's what will fuel your energy. And it's simple. I've used this example before, but here's how I think about life: it's like a vacation, and

Heaven is like going home. I know I'm going someday, but I freaking love it here on Earth. This is one badass vacation. So, I'm doing what I can to enjoy.

Keep in mind that this does not necessarily come easily to me. I don't always "live each day like it's my last." I get caught up in drama and my ever-growing to-do list and some of the b.s. from everyday life. But then I remember that none of that shit really matters. And I don't actually have to live each day like it's my last. I just need to keep doing the best I can. To love my people and to do what makes me happy.

That, to me, is what life is about. That's happiness.

Anything else just gets in the way of it—makes it unnecessarily complicated. It's meant for you. You get to have it. Focus on what you can do—what you're good at, what comes naturally and that you enjoy. Do the things that make you happy.

Can you really find your happiness in 10 weeks?

YES! You absolutely can. Here's the thing: you can change every single thing in your life with one perspective shift. One new idea, one change. And that can happen in way less time. In fact, it can happen in an instant.

Everyone is different. But when you put the ownership of your happiness on you, when you turn the responsibility inward instead of outward, you can get there.

I've definitely put other people in charge of my happiness at different times in my life. And every single time, I come back to the realization that it's up to me. Most of the time, I'm pretty annoyed by this realization, but it's true.

And honestly, the first step for most of us is to get clear on what happiness even means.

How do you define it?

The definition you're working with is probably old, untrue or not even yours.

That's a problem with a pretty easy solution: redefine what happiness means to you.

What's your daily routine? What actions do you take to feel good and to be happy?

Ha! I've never been great with structure or routine. And that part of me feels even more lost since becoming a mom. One of the things I teach in my *Laugh More, Live Louder* course is the importance of creating some kind of success structure but being flexible with it and really matching your action to your energy. Do what feels good.

One thing I do pretty consistently is start my morning with a big glass of lemon water (12oz or so) and I'm pretty consistent with my supplements—they just differ based on what I'm focusing on.

So for me, I like to feel strong in my body. Some days, that means taking my dog for a walk (she's a beast!!!). Some days, it means yoga; some days, it means lifting weights; and some days, it means chasing my kiddo. The activity itself doesn't really matter—I just want to feel my body being strong.

My meditation practice is like that, too. Sometimes, it's listening to something I've downloaded or one of the Oprah & Deepak 21-day meditations before bed or when I first wake up.

Sometimes, it's just going for a walk outside by myself and getting quiet. Sometimes, it's taking a long, hot shower and just letting my brain go.

I also love journaling, but that comes in waves. I do that mostly when I'm trying to get clear on or unstuck with something.

My gratitude practice is thanking God every night for that day, for all that's working in my life and the people I love.

There are a lot of tools and strategies that I know, love and turn to regularly. I trust that I'll pull the right one out when I need it and that it's okay to not do all the things all the time. I just do what I want and need in that moment.

I also try to eat healthfully, drink lots of water and read things that I find interesting in magazines or books…but I do tend to get sucked down the virtual rabbit hole at times, which I always regret after!!!

How did you get started with writing?

I've always loved to write. I love to read. I love stories. Writing a book has been a long time dream for me. But it's one I turned off back in undergrad after one of my creative writing professors spent much of the semester redlining my papers and telling me I was awful at it.

Which, in all honesty, ended up being okay because I dove into psychology. Human behavior and how the brain works—I find all of that fascinating.

Then, when I was learning about things to help my body as I was dealing with a diagnosis of unexplained infertility, I became fascinated with the role food plays in how we think and feel.

Now, I get to write about all of that in a way I truly believe can be really helpful to people.

Did you always see yourself doing what you're doing now?

Ten years ago, I did not see myself here, which is why I think it's so, so important to dream your dream, build out that vision, and then just take it one step at a time, really being open to wherever each step takes you.

My path to here was a windy one. I never would've thought of myself as a health and happiness expert. I started my career as a traditional psychotherapist working with kids and adults on coping with things like anxiety, mood and attention struggles.

I noticed time and time again that people were mostly just talking about the "problem." And most of the time, that "problem" was them. If you see yourself as the problem or your people (family, friends, teachers, etc.) are pointing to you as the problem, then you feel like you have to change who you are.

But in my mind, that's backwards. It's not about changing who you are; it's about being clear on who you are, accepting it and learning to leverage your unique combo of strengths and gifts.

Focusing on the problem and all that's not working is pretty much a guaranteed way to feel like shit. Every single person is dealing with their own stuff. And every single person has things they're good at and things they're not good at. That's just it.

Yet, that's not how we approach life. We're taught to focus on the wrong things. I spent a lot of time in middle school and high school focusing on math—I had to stay after school and get help with it. Not my strength and I hated it. That hasn't changed. And I'm doing just fine. Yet, for a lot of years, I focused on improving an area that I never got great in, don't really use that much now and quite honestly, just made me feel really bad about myself.

I'm not alone in this. People are constantly trying to change themselves to fit into something they're just not meant to fit into. People are a lot happier when they stop doing that, and when they can see the value they bring to the table and really learn to leverage their strengths and interests.

Not just happier, but way more productive and successful. It's a mistake I see with kids in school and with adults in their careers. If we could focus on teaching people to change the systems or structures they're using or the environments they're in instead of who they are, the world would be a much happier (more productive and successful) place.

It's so simple and so obvious, but so few people are doing it (or have any idea how). One of the reasons I wrote *Happiness Happens* is to help people get reconnected to who they are and grounded in that so they can stop feeling bad about themselves and focus on making the changes they actually need to make to be happy.

How did your personal journey inspire your work?

My husband and I were married in 2007, wanted to have kids right away but instead, we were stuck in this 7-year cycle of unexplained infertility.

As I started to make changes in my life to help get pregnant— mostly around how I was taking care of my body—all these things started to shift for me. I started to feel better, and look at things differently. Bottom line was that I felt happier about who I was and how I was living.

That opened the door for me to dream my new dream: Balance & Thrive. I didn't give up on having a baby—I just needed to find a way to do that and not be consumed by it. This was how I found my way to "be happy anyway." Doing that opened the doors for me to be messy and imperfect. And to be okay with life being hard sometimes, but not letting that be the deciding factor in who I was being or how I was living.

I genuinely believe that all any of us wants is to be happy. It's really just the bottom line. We overcomplicate it. When we just bring it back to this simple thing that we want, we can find different and much easier ways to make happiness happen.

I just want to bring it back to the basics without all the fluff. We all want to be happy. Happiness is a simple thing. You can have it regardless of what's happening in your life. And it truly comes from you being good with who you are and how you're living. *That's it!*

What's next?

More writing, for sure. And continuing to expand on the *Laugh More, Live Louder* course by adding in some guest expert interviews. Maybe a podcast, more speaking and fun live events. And there are some exciting collaborations on the horizon, too.

Definitely enjoying this last year of total freedom and flexibility with my kiddo before he starts preschool next year. And I have some things I'm excited about that I'll share as they come together! Every time you reach a new level, you have to take a step back and check back in with yourself to see how you've changed, who you are now and what you want in this moment. I'm getting ready to do that again now that I'm wrapping up this first book, and I'm excited for what's to come.

I imagine I'll come up with a plan and God will give me a version of it that I never even could've imagined…at least, that seems to be what keeps happening ;). And so far, it's worked out pretty great!

Stay tuned…

Acknowledgments

I've been fortunate to be surrounded by amazing people in my life. People who supported me when life felt especially messy and those same people who are here with me now to enjoy the other side of the mess. I have to thank some of these core people because without them, this book would definitely not have happened.

My parents have been a source of support and guidance throughout my whole life. Their love and acceptance created the homebase that was always safe for me to come back to. My mom's perspective and my dad's life lessons are the foundation for how I live and what I teach.

My mom is an amazing sounding board and I'm grateful that she's helped me develop so many of my ideas. There aren't many words I've written that she hasn't talked through with me. My dad taught me how to be independent and work hard. I plan and follow through on what I say because he taught me to do so. And both nurtured my creativity in very valuable, yet very different ways.

My sister who is one of the kindest people I know. She has a heart of gold and a laugh that lights up a room. She is one of my most favorite people and I am grateful to know her, and especially to call her my sister. A few years ago, following devastating news after IVF didn't work and there were no eggs to try again, she made one of the most generous offers one woman can make to another and she did it in one of the most understated and selfless ways. Having a human like that in your corner makes hard things easier and good things even better.

Suz, my aunt, who truly makes this world a better place simply by being in it. She is so thoughtful and generous. I love that she has always been, and continues to be, such a fundamental person in my life. She is also the first person to let me watch what ended up being my all-time favorite movie *Dirty Dancing*. I know that having an aunt like that—who loves you and lets you do the things your parents won't—is one of the key ingredients to happiness.

Mark, my hubby. My road dog and life partner. I truly don't know who (or where) I'd be without you. You show me every single day what love is. And that love gives me the courage to take risks and go for my dreams. You also don't let me get too caught up in the drama of life. You're quick to call me on my shit and you remind me to focus on the things that actually matter. You live the words in this book more naturally than anyone I know. Thank you for leading by example.

And to my sweet, sweet baby boy. Thank you for letting me be your mom and for being my real-life proof that miracles, in fact, do happen. I am a better human because of you. And you make my heart happier than words can ever even begin to describe.

I also have to thank my amazing clients. Each and every one of you have inspired me with your journey. I feel grateful to know you and to have witnessed the massive transformation you've made. Seeing you cut through all the stuff so you can be you and do your thing is awesome. It's what makes this work that I do meaningful. You give it purpose and fuel me forward. And you truly make this world a better place. Thank you, thank you, thank you!

Deb Bailey, my book writing coach. Who helped me to navigate this journey and held me accountable so that I'd get this book out of my head and into your hands. You showed me the way to make my dream happen—that's priceless, and I thank you a million times over for that. And thank you to Melissa Cassera for making the connection!

Thank you to my editor and book designer for honing in on all the details, putting on those important finishing touches and making this book look absolutely amazing!

Last but not least, thank you to Stella, my bullmastiff. You ate (quite literally) some pieces that needed to go and challenged me to not completely lose my shit as I sat back down to create something new and better than before. Now, if you could please stop eating all of the things, that would be great!

About the Author

Emily Capuria, LISW-S, CHHC is a writer, speaker and coach who is passionate about redefining happiness and showing people how easily accessible it is once you shift your definition and reconnect with who you truly are.

Emily has a Bachelor's degree in Psychology from the University of Kentucky and a Master's degree in Social Work from Cleveland State University. Prior to becoming a coach, she worked in community mental health, where she used a strengths-based, solution-focused framework to help children, adults and families learn to cope with challenges relating to anxiety, mood and attention.

Emily now pairs mindset and action strategies with a holistic approach to offer people a unique path to align who they are and what they want, with how they live. Her clients include high achieving professionals, start up entrepreneurs, busy parents and anyone committed to making changes in their lives. She has also coached in corporate wellness programs to support employee stress reduction, work/life balance, job satisfaction and productivity.

Emily is the creator of the, Laugh More, Live Louder Course, which helps people to map out what's next and take the steps to make it happen. She is also the founder of Balance & Thrive, a business that offers a holistic approach to living a happy, fulfilling life. Learn more at balancethrive.com.

Emily lives in Cleveland, OH with her family. When she's not coaching and writing, she's trying to keep up with her puppy/toddler tag team, and enjoying time with family and friends. She especially loves '90s hip hop and country music (kitchen dance parties, anyone?), the south Jersey Shore and pretty much all books. She also pretends to love working out and cooking, but the truth is, she mostly just loves feeling strong and eating good food ;).

CPSIA information can be obtained
at www.ICGtesting.com
Printed in the USA
BVHW012126110122
626053BV00002B/69